Health Essentials

Flower Remedies

Christine Wildwood is an experienced Bach Flower Practitioner and aromatherapist. As well as several books on aromatherapy, she has written a number of magazine articles on health-related subjects. She also conducts workshops on aromatherapy, deep relaxation, and meditation. The author lives in South Wales and runs a very popular holistic health practice from her home.

The Health Essentials Series

There is a growing number of people who find themselves attracted to holistic or alternative therapies and natural approaches to maintaining optimum health and vitality. The *Health Essentials* series is designed to help the newcomer by presenting high quality introductions to all the main complementary health subjects. Each book presents all the essential information on each therapy, explaining what it is, how it works and what it can do for the reader. Advice is also given, where possible, on how to begin using the therapy at home, together with comprehensive lists of courses and classes available worldwide.

The *Health Essentials* titles are all written by practising experts in their fields. Exceptionally clear and concise, each text is supported by attractive illustrations.

Series Medical Consultant
Dr. John Cosh MD, FRCP

In the same series

Acupuncture by Peter Mole
Alexander Technique by Richard Brennan
Aromatherapy by Christine Wildwood
Ayurveda by Scott Gerson
Chi Kung by James MacRitchie
Chinese Medicine by Tom Williams
Colour Therapy by Pauline Wills
Herbal Medicine by Vicki Pitman
Kinesiology by Ann Holdway
Massage by Stewart Mitchell
Reflexology by Inge Dougans with Suzanne Ellis
Shiatsu by Elaine Liechti
Skin and Body Care by Sidra Shaukat
Spiritual Healing by Jack Angelo
Vitamin Guide by Hasnain Walji

Health Essentials

FLOWER REMEDIES

Natural Healing
with Flower Essences

CHRISTINE WILDWOOD

ELEMENT
Shaftesbury, Dorset ● Rockport, Massachusetts

© Christine Wildwood 1992, 1995

First published in Great Britain in 1992 by
Element Books Limited
Shaftesbury, Dorset SP7 8BP

Published in the USA in 1992 by
Element Books, Inc
42 Broadway, Rockport, MA 01966

Published in Australia in 1995 by
Element Books Limited
for Jacaranda Wiley Limited
33 Park Road, Milton, Brisbane 4064

Reprinted 1995

Cover illustration by Sally Townsend
Cover design by Max Fairbrother
Designed by Nancy Lawrence
Typeset by Falcon Typographic Art Ltd, Edinburgh
Printed and bound in Great Britain by
Biddles Limited, Guildford & King's Lynn

British Library Cataloguing in Publication Data
available

Library of Congress Cataloging in Publication Data
available

ISBN 1–85230–336–0

Note from the Publisher
Any information given in any book in the *Health Essentials* series is
not intended to be taken as a replacement for medical advice. Any
person with a condition requiring medical attention should consult
a qualified medical practitioner or suitable therapist.

Contents

Acknowledgements

With many thanks to all at Mount Vernon and to everyone else who contributed in some way to the birth of this book. And to Dr Edward Bach whose shining spirit lives on through his work.

1

What are the Bach Flower Remedies?

Mount Vernon, an unpretentious little house and pretty garden in Oxfordshire, England, is the source of an intriguing system of healing known as Bach Flower Therapy. In this method, certain wild flowers are selected for their special ability to treat the personality and distressing emotions of the sufferer rather than the physical symptoms of illness.

The thirty-eight Remedies which comprise the Bach Flower pharmacopoeia have been prepared at Mount Vernon for nearly sixty years. Indeed, the present trustees of the work continue to collect wild flowers from the same locations, and use the original methods of preparation discovered in the 1930s by the visionary physician, Dr Edward Bach.

The simple beauty of the house, also known as the Bach Centre, combined with the unaffected personality of Bach himself, is perfectly mirrored in the gentle Flower Remedies which have become quietly renowned throughout the world. Mount Vernon was Bach's home for the last years of his life. It was here that he perfected his work, and from here that he departed, satisfied in the knowledge that his mission on Earth had been accomplished.

In order that we may begin to understand the Bach system, we need to take a look at the philosophy behind it. Although we shall expound on this in subsequent chapters, let us begin with Bach's quest for a method of treatment which would embrace the mind and spirit of the person – an approach calling for no medical training, simply a natural sensitivity and feeling for others.

By 1930, Edward Bach, then aged 43, had attained eminence as a consultant, bacteriologist, and homoeopath. Indeed, his name

1

is perpetuated by the seven Bach Nosodes which he discovered, and which are still used to this day in homoeopathic medicine. (Nosodes are homoeopathic remedies prepared from substances of pathological origin.) Much to the chagrin of the British medical establishment, however, he was inspired (for there is no other word for it) to give up his lucrative London practice to seek a completely new form of healing, a totally benign method which would harm neither man nor beast. He became convinced that poisonous substances of animal, plant or mineral origin should play no part in healing – even when used in infinitesimal doses as in homoeopathy.

Bach's homoeopathic background had, however, opened the doors of his perception to the reality of *vibrational* healing. He was aware that highly diluted medicinal substances, so diluted that the original material cannot be detected in the laboratory, can trigger a powerful healing effect in the body. This knowledge was to influence the development of his own system of healing.

Equally important to Bach was the realization that long continued stress resulting from emotions such as anger, fear or worry lowered a person's resistance to disease. The body would then become prey to all manner of infection or illness, whether it be a cold, shingles, a digestive upset or something much more serious. At the same time, he observed that an individual's emotional outlook influenced the course, severity, and duration of their disease. Moreover, he noticed that people suffering from the same disease and sharing similar personalities responded well to a particular remedy, but that others of a different temperament needed other treatment, although they were suffering from the same physical complaint. Thus Bach's axiom became: Take no notice of the disease, think only of the personality of the one in distress. According to Bach, disease is a consolidation of a mental state, and in this view, he was sharing the opinion of Plato as well as that of many contemporary practitioners of holistic medicine.

Although highly intelligent and with a sound scientific background, Bach never lost touch with his spiritual nature. He was essentially a 'heart man', guided by intuition, or what some might call divine inspiration. He believed strongly that the key to the art of true healing lay not in the laboratory but within the plant kingdom, and that these special plants would be found growing wild, nurtured by the living Earth and energized by the synergy of fresh air, water, and sunlight.

Immediately after leaving London, Bach settled down in a village near Betws-y-Coed in North Wales. Living close to nature, his innate sensitivity blossomed fully. He was already aware of his gift of healing, for many times in the past he had suddenly felt the impulse to lay his hand on a patient's arm or shoulder and that person would feel a rush of healing energy flooding their body. Whilst in Wales, however, his sensitivity became so highly developed that he had merely to place a petal on his tongue or hold his hand over a flowering plant to be aware of its effects on the mind, body, and spirit. Later he was to gain his knowledge in a different way: for some days before the discovery of a healing flower he experienced in himself, in a magnified form, the distressing state of mind for which that particular flower was a remedy. Indeed, he suffered intensely in his quest, both physically and mentally.

According to Bach, certain flowers are of a 'higher order' and hold a greater power than those ordinary medicinal plants which heal the body from a biochemical level. The true healing plants, he believed, address disharmony within the mental and spiritual aspects of our being. They transmute negative emotions such as fear, melancholy, and hatred into courage, joy, and love; and in this manner, they correct the *cause* of our ills. The Flower Remedies do not simply buffer the effects of a turbulent perception as is the case with some mind-bending substances. Instead they act as a gentle catalyst, generating change from within.

Just how they achieve this, no one really knows for certain. Their mode of action may be similar to other vibrational healing methods (see Chapter 2), particularly the homoeopathic 'mentals' which are prescribed according to the temperament of the individual, not his or her physical symptoms. As Bach puts it:

> The remedies cure, not by attacking the disease, but by flooding our bodies with the beautiful vibrations of our Higher Nature, in the presence of which, disease melts away as snow in the sunshine.[1]

A SIMPLE METHOD OF POTENTIZATION

> Let not the simplicity of this method deter you from its use, for you will find the further your researches advance, the greater you will realise the simplicity of all creation.[2]

While living in Wales, Bach would walk through the lush green meadows, the early-morning dew still heavy on the ground. It occurred to him that each dew-drop must contain some of the properties of the plant upon which it rested. He decided to test this theory by collecting the dew from certain flowers and trying it out on himself. Through his finely developed senses, he found that the dew held a definite power of some kind. Moreover, dew collected from flowers exposed to sunlight was far more potent than that collected from flowers growing in the shade. He also found that the essential energies of a plant were concentrated in the flower at full maturity, that is, when it has reached its peak of perfection and is about to fall.

Having proved to himself that sun-warmed dew absorbed the properties of the plant upon which it rested, he set himself the task of finding a simple technique for capturing the flower energies (collecting dew proved to be too time-consuming). He sought a method which would neither destroy nor damage the plant itself, and in fact, devised two methods of extraction – or 'potentization' as he preferred to call it – the Sun Method and the Boiling Method.

In the Sun Method, the best flower heads are carefully picked. These are put in a thin, clear glass or crystal bowl filled with spring water. The bowl is then placed on the ground (near the parent plants) where it is exposed to strong sunlight for a few hours – or until the healing energy of the blooms is transferred to the water. Afterwards, the flowers are carefully removed with a twig or leaf from the Remedy plant, thus avoiding human contact with the vitalized water or 'essence'. The essence is then poured into bottles half-filled with brandy, which acts as a preservative, and labelled 'Mother Tincture'.

A few years later, as his work developed, Bach realized that certain blooms, such as **Star of Bethlehem**, **Willow** and **Elm**, required a stronger method of extraction, though he did not explain why. It was for these flowers that he devised the Boiling Method.

In this process, plant material (buds, cones, or flowers) is placed in an enamel pan of spring water and simmered for half-an-hour. Afterwards, the pan is covered and left to cool. When cold, the essence is filtered and, as in the previous method, preserved in equal quantities of brandy and labelled 'Mother Tincture'.

The next stage in the preparation, whether using the Sun or the Boiling Method, is to dilute the Mother Tincture in a further quantity of brandy. This bottle is labelled 'Stock Concentrate', and it is in this form that the Remedies are usually sold. Although the Stock is a dilution of the original tincture, it is nevertheless considered to be a concentrated Remedy because it requires further dilution in spring water before administration (see Chapter 5).

Of the thirty-eight Flower Remedies, two are a little different because they are not prepared from European wild flowers. These are **Rock Water** (potentized spring water) and **Cerato** which is a cultivated plant native to the Himalayas.

Bach's choice of **Rock Water** as a Remedy is fairly easy to understand since it is prepared from natural spring water already vitalized by the energies of the Earth (see page 69). But why he should have gone against the grain in choosing the ornamental **Cerato** as a Flower Remedy is anyone's guess. Julian Barnard, author of several books on the Bach Remedies, puts forward an interesting theory: that the plant both poses the question and provides the answer. **Cerato** is for those who suffer from uncertainty!

FLOWER REMEDIES IN PRACTICE

Those unfamiliar with the principles of homoeopathy, which the Flower Remedies mimic to a degree, may find it difficult to accept that so little can do so much. As we have gleaned so far, the Flower Remedies represent plant energy, rather than measurable quantities of a therapeutic substance. Therefore, the Remedies could be described as a form of energy medicine, or spiritual healing, accessible to everyone.

The Remedies are prepared from non-poisonous flowers and unpolluted water, and so unlike drugs or herbal remedies proper, an 'overdose' would be totally harmless. The Remedies are non-addictive and can be taken by adults, children, and infants alike. Furthermore, many Bach users have found the Remedies beneficial to animals – and even plants – which, of course, dispels the placebo myth so often espoused by sceptics.

In order that we may use the Flower Remedies successfully, we need to move away from the habit of thinking in terms of physical symptoms. Simply because a Flower Remedy has helped a friend's eczema as well as her anxiety, it does not follow that the same prescription will help your skin problem. It is important to choose the correct Remedy, or combination of Remedies, to match your specific emotional needs.

As we have seen, Bach recognized thirty-eight healing flowers, one for each of the most common negative states of mind which darken our perception. Each Remedy transmutes the negative outlook into its opposite or positive aspect. **Holly**, for example, is the Remedy for those who harbour hatred, envy, or suspicion. A course of this Remedy will enable such a person to give without wanting anything in return, and to rejoice in the good fortune of others.

Or consider the **Vine** type: domineering, inflexible, and sometimes ruthlessly ambitious. A course of **Vine** will bring out the positive side of such a personality such as seen in the strong but loving leader; a person who can inspire others.

Let us take an example from real life. Who but a Bach Flower user would believe that the delicate pink blossom of the **Red Chestnut** tree could help those who are habitually over-anxious for the welfare of their loved ones?

I was quite recently reminded of the transmuting energy of this particular Remedy when Mary came to see me. She was in a depressed and anxious state over the plight of her nephew, Peter, a young soldier serving in the Gulf during the recent conflict. She feared for his safety: 'What if he's killed, how would my sister live with the pain? If only I could have talked him out of joining the army . . . He must be so afraid, so *alone* . . . what on earth can I do to help him?'

Within a few days of taking the Remedy, Mary telephoned to tell me how much calmer she was feeling and, more importantly, that she had been able to send out thoughts of safety and love to Peter. 'He's a man after all', she said, 'so he's entitled to choose the path of his own life, no matter how dangerous.'

Then there was Mark, a timid man who lacked confidence and always anticipated failure. The certainty of failure had become ingrained, reinforced by past experiences.

At the age of thirty-seven he was about to take his driving test for the 'umpteenth' time: 'It's no good,' he said, 'I'm not a driver, I don't suppose I'll ever pass. I don't know why I continue to waste my money.'

Mark was a typical **Larch** type. The drooping, languid appearance of the branches of this tree mirrors the mental state for which the Remedy is indicated – lack of confidence and despondency. I must admit, Mark did fail the test which was imminent, but two months later, having taken the Remedy for several weeks, he passed – a miracle as far as he was concerned!

More often than not, however, few people are as true to type as these examples have suggested. Most require a mixture of Flower Remedies to deal with the various negative aspects that may be predominant, especially in cases of deep-rooted physical and emotional disharmony (see Chapters 3 and 6).

COMPLEMENTARY AND PREVENTATIVE

Although Bach was an idealist, he was not unrealistic. He would have been the first to employ other forms of treatment when necessary to support the action of the Flower Remedies.

The philosophy of holism holds that the mind, body, and spirit are interrelated, and that whatever affects one aspect, affects the whole. It is a fact of life that few people do enough to help themselves by living as healthily as they could. The person who exists on junk food, smokes heavily, and rarely leaves the armchair cannot expect the Remedies to work wonders on the physical level – though the Remedies might trigger in that person a desire for change. However, even Dr Bach himself – though aware of the importance of a healthy lifestyle and diet – did not always adhere to this principle. In fact, it would be no exaggeration to suggest that self-neglect through over-work and cigarette smoking contributed to his own poor health and early death.

The Bach Flower Remedies are a wonderful adjunct to all other forms of treatment, be it allopathy (orthodox medicine), homoeopathy, herbalism, acupuncture, aromatherapy, and such like. They work on the mental/spiritual level and will not interfere with any other means of healing the body – in fact, they enhance other forms of treatment.

In my own experience as an aromatherapist, the Flower Remedies help release ingrained fear and tension which often manifest as cold, painful, or over-sensitive areas in the body – the feet, solar plexus, shoulders or buttocks, for example. The Remedies appear to hasten the healing process, especially in those who find it extremely difficult to let go.

The Bach Remedies reign supreme in the area of preventative treatment. Indeed, it is far better to use them in this manner than to wait until you are ill. The Remedies help us cope with the ups and downs of life. They affect the emotions, which in turn affect the body. If you correct a distressing state of mind, it becomes possible to forestall a physical disturbance before it has time to manifest as illness.

ARE THERE MORE REMEDIES TO BE FOUND?

Even though Bach considered his work to be complete, it would be unrealistic to suggest that no other flowers of a 'higher order' exist. In fact, you may have come across other flower remedies known as 'flower essences' prepared by the Bach method. While these remedies are no doubt efficacious, they should not be confused with the Bach Flower Remedies, nor with aromatic extractions known as essential oils, also sometimes called 'essences', as used in aromatherapy and perfumery.

Some other flower essences are based on herbal remedies proper: that is to say, in addition to their physiological effects, they are believed to influence certain mental states. The Bach Remedies deal *solely* with negative states of mind. **Mimulus**, for example, though it may have medicinal properties if used as a herb tea, or even perhaps as a homoeopathic remedy, when taken as a Bach Remedy deals with fear and anxiety. It has no *direct* influence on the body. However, by transmuting fear and anxiety into their positive aspects of courage and understanding, healing on a physical level may indeed follow. Thus the Bach Remedies heal the body *indirectly*.

On first acquaintance with the Bach system, it may be difficult to accept that there are only thirty-eight negative states of mind – surely there must be many more? For instance, there is no specific Remedy for anger. According to John Ramsell and Judy Howard of the Bach Centre, anger and other uncategorized states of mind represent sub-headings, as it were. They are states that can be caused or created by any manner of related problems. We therefore need to look deeper and to begin by determining *how* or *why* any predominant condition of mind manifests. Anger is often associated with hatred or envy, but can equally be caused by frustration, worry, resentment, or any other conditioned state of mind. So we need to ask ourselves, or the person for whom we are prescribing, what is the *cause* of this anger? In other words, it is by coming down to basics that the correct Remedy, or mixture of Remedies, will become apparent.

Although I occasionally use other flower essences, I have yet to be stumped by an 'uncategorized' state of mind. No matter what the person may be suffering from, there is always a Bach Flower Remedy to suit the individual's personality and changing pattern of mood.

TRAINING IN BACH FLOWER THERAPY

There is no professional qualification in Bach Flower Therapy. Most practitioners are qualified in some other form of therapy and employ the Bach Remedies as an adjunct to their work. Dr Bach intended this treatment to be a simple self-help measure available to people from all walks of life. Therefore, the books and leaflets available have always been considered sufficient in themselves. The Bach Remedies are never advertised but, nevertheless, talks and seminars are given by individuals intent on 'spreading the word'. You may find information about such talks on notice boards of health food shops, natural health clinics and public libraries – or contact the Bach Centre (page 119).

If you intend to set yourself up as a Bach Flower practitioner, it would be of enormous benefit to broaden your knowledge by gaining some counselling skills and a recognized counselling qualification. Do find out about courses in your area.

BACH THE COMPOSER OR 'BATCH'?

Visitors to Mount Vernon will have heard the Doctor's name pronounced as 'Batch'. Bach's family came from Wales where *bach* means 'little' or 'dear', and is pronounced in the guttural way as in Bach the composer. However, Bach began his medical training in England where most of his fellow students were English and tended to pronounce (or mispronounce!) his name as 'Batch'; and by this name he has been known ever since – at least at Mount Vernon.

BUYING THE REMEDIES

The Stock Concentrates may be obtained from many health shops, some chemists, or by mail order (see Useful Addresses, page 119).

2

How do the Remedies Work?

UNTIL VERY RECENTLY, a non-esoteric explanation for the Remedies' mode of action would have appeared inconceivable. Indeed, authors have tended to steer clear of the harsh light of scientific reason in favour of the soft shadows of spiritual reflection. At last, however, with the wonderful awakening of science in the form of quantum physics and the development of mindbody medicine, an equalized explanation may be possible.

Before we can begin to understand how the Remedies work, we need to move away from the materialistic bias. Firstly we shall consider the possibility of a universal intelligence or life-force. Secondly we shall explore the ancient concept that the body is not so much a solid sculpture, but a flowing river. Thirdly we shall consider the components of the life-flow – the sub-atomic particles best described as energy or vibration. And finally we shall embrace the whole of creation in the realization that far from being separate observers of the universe, we are in fact an intricate part of its fabric, a *vibrating* aspect of the whole.

THE LIFE-FORCE

The doctrine of materialism holds that the body, and indeed all life, is essentially biochemical in nature and that the reality of the mind is merely a function of matter. But can we really reduce the human being to the level of chemicals? Let us consider for a moment the remarkable co-ordination and synergistic action of our physiology.

We tend to view the body as a machine composed of many parts and functions operating in separate compartments, when in fact, like the Earth's eco-systems, everything is invisibly linked. At any one time we breathe, eat, talk, think, digest our food, fight off infection, renew our cells, and much more besides. Blood cells, for example, rush to the site of a wound and begin to form a clot. These cells have not travelled there by chance, they actually 'know' where to go and what to do when they arrive. Indeed, every activity within the organism is animated by an invisible and seemingly intelligent force, a force which is involved with the whole of us on all levels, not just the biochemical. In the words of physician Dr Deepak Chopra: 'Intelligence makes the difference between a house designed by an architect and a pile of bricks.' Or to consider it another way, at death, the chemicals are still present, but something has gone.

THE SCULPTURE OR THE RIVER?

The Greek philosopher Heraclitus of Ephesus believed in a world of perpetual change, of eternal 'becoming'. He made the interesting observation, 'you cannot step into the same river twice' (because the river is constantly flowing). Likewise, according to Dr Chopra, if we could see the body the way it really is, we would never see the same body twice. Far from being a solid mass, the body is in a state of constant change. The skeleton, for instance, may seem solid, yet the bones we have today were not there three months ago. Cells of the body are constantly being replaced. We make a new liver every six weeks, a new skin every month, and a new stomach lining every four days. In fact, ninety-eight percent of the atoms in our body were not there a year ago. So the body we can see and touch is, in reality, a stream of energy. But what of mind?

For many centuries philosophers have contemplated the nature of mind. Some have concluded that mind is a phenomenon apart from physical reality, an aspect of the immortal spirit of the individual. Others have decided that mind is merely a function of the brain – a fiction, medically speaking. Although we may never know the absolute truth, modern physics has begun to move closer towards understanding the nature of mind.

In the 1970s, a series of important discoveries began which centred on a new class of minute chemicals called neuro-transmitters and neuro-peptides. These chemicals were considered revolutionary at the time because they proved that the nerves did not work electrically like a telegraph system, as had been believed, but that nerve impulses were chemical in nature. As Dr Chopra puts it:

> The arrival of neuro-transmitters on the scene makes the interaction of mind and matter far more mobile and flowing than ever before — far closer to a model of a river. They also help fill the gap that apparently separates mind and body, one of the deepest mysteries man has faced since he began to consider what he is.[3]

Amazingly, it appears that the non-material thought gives rise to the neuro-chemicals. 'To think', says Chopra, 'is to practise brain chemistry, promoting a cascade of responses throughout the body.'

Another enthralling discovery which lends credence to the reality of 'mind over matter' is that receptors for neuro-chemicals are to be found in other parts of the body such as the skin, and on cells in the immune system called monocytes. These 'intelligent' blood cells circulate freely throughout the body, apparently sending and receiving messages just as diverse as those in the central nervous system. This means that if, when we are happy, depressed, angry, in love, or whatever, we produce brain chemicals in various parts of the body, then those parts must also be happy, depressed, angry, or in love. Moreover (as if this were not astonishing enough), insulin, a hormone always associated with the pancreas, is now known to be produced in the brain as well, just as brain chemicals such as transferon and CCK are produced in the stomach. Without doubt, the flowing, interrelated *bodymind* is a reality.

VIBRATION

A well-known mathematical formula, Bell's Theorem, formulated in 1964 by Irish physicist John Bell, holds that the reality of the universe is an interconnected whole wherein all objects and events respond to one another's changes in state. British astronomer Sir Arthur Eddington went so far as to conclude that an *intelligent* force holds the universe together: 'The stuff of the world is mind stuff'. More recently, theorists such as British physicist, David Bohm, have reached a similar conclusion: that there is an 'invisible field' holding all of reality together, a field that possesses the property of knowing what is happening everywhere at once. This is the quantum mechanical world, a world beyond the atom, the proton, electron and quark – all of which can be broken down into smaller particles (at least in theory) and therefore occupy space. Whatever it is that shapes the universe and bestows it with life is non-material – it takes up no space. It is believed, therefore, that the quantum, or sub-atomic world is that of energy or vibration, and it is at this point of realization that the marriage of science and mysticism takes place. Modern physics, in tune with Eastern mysticism, pictures the universe as à continuous, dancing, and vibrating web of life.

EMBRACING THE WHOLE

At the quantum level, matter, from a crystal to a human being, is essentially energy or vibration. In this realm, there is no distinction between animate and inanimate, between spirit and matter. We perceive ourselves as separate from other things because different kinds of matter and energy such as water, rock, and sentient life-forms vibrate at different frequencies. Mind energy, for instance, vibrates so fast that it appears to be invisible, whereas rock vibrates so slowly that we are unaware of its essential dynamism. Likewise, humans are 'deaf' to high and low frequency sounds, but this does not mean we cannot be affected by them.

In the view of German physicist Werner Heisenberg, if we set a single strand of the cosmic web in vibration we affect the whole:

> The world thus appears as a complicated tissue of events in which connections of different kinds alternate or overlap or combine and thereby determine the texture of the whole.[4]

In the light of all this, we can now take a look at the mode of action of the Bach Flower Remedies.

HEALING VIBRATIONS

Bach believed that the flowers used for the Remedies were of a 'higher order'. Unlike medicinal herbs which vibrate at a similar frequency to that of matter, the Flower Remedies are in tune with the finer frequencies of the mind/spirit. By flooding our energy field (see page 15) with these higher frequencies, our whole being (the mind-body-spirit) becomes aligned with the cosmic flow. The discordant notes of negative emotion, which slow down our vibrations and make us feel unwell, are brought into harmony. As Bach himself said: 'The human being becomes very much himself again at a point where he had ceased to be quite himself.'

There are many other healing methods which act on the subtle or vibrational level: for example, homoeopathy, spiritual healing, colour healing, gem therapy, music therapy, and aromatherapy, although this last does include massage to enhance the ethereal or vibrational influence of the aromatic plant oils.

In order that we may glean further insight into the efficacy, or otherwise, of vibrational healing substances, let us return to the world of science. Although the following account concerns itself with the principles of homoeopathy, it is also relevant to the mode of action of the Bach Flower Remedies in that infinitesimal quantities are used.

In 1987, a French immunobiologist shook the foundations of the non-quantum medical establishment when he proved that certain highly diluted substances could be as potent as vastly greater quantities of the same substance. In laboratory tests, Dr Jacques Benveniste demonstrated that living cells could be influenced by Immunoglobulin E in dilutions so high that it was unlikely that a single molecule remained in the test solution .

Despite the fact that Benveniste's discovery defied the laws of materialism, he duplicated the experiment seventy times, and asked other scientists to repeat it in Israel, Canada and Italy – all came up with the same result.

Even though Benveniste's findings were published in the June 1988 edition of *Nature* (a British journal), the editors frankly declared their disbelief. Benveniste was lending credence to the methods of homoeopathy which employs minute amounts of antagonistic substances to heal the body. A month after publishing the results of the experiment, *Nature* sent a team of experts to France to view Benveniste's findings. Unfortunately, he was unable consistently to duplicate his results; some trials worked, others did not. Quick off the mark, *Nature* condemned Benveniste's work, calling his results a 'delusion' and ignoring the fact that the original paper had been signed by twelve other researchers in four countries.

In view of what we have already discovered about the nature of mind, is it possible that the negative vibrations emanating from the sceptical onlookers could actually have hampered the trials? Incidentally, *Nature* failed to comment on the experiments which did work. It appears that certain members of the medical establishment are most reluctant to enter into the realms of quantum reality.

THE AURA

As we have already seen, vibrational healing methods such as homoeopathy and the Bach Flower Remedies act at a subtle level. Many therapists working with these remedies believe that the healing effect is triggered in the human energy field, or aura, which surrounds and interpenetrates the physical aspect. From this field, which is essentially a thought-form, the healing effect of the remedies filters 'inwards', as it were, to the physical level. In contrast, material medicines such as herbs and drugs move 'outwards' from the physical level, eventually affecting the aura.

Although psychics describe the aura differently, according to their own level of psychic perception, it is generally agreed that the aura is a rainbow emanation (some sensitives can see its colours) surrounding the body. The aura is composed of at least three, and possibly seven, 'layers' of energy, each layer vibrating at a different frequency. The physical body or matter vibrates at the slowest or densest frequency, while the subtle body, like electricity, vibrates much faster, which is why we are usually unaware of its existence. The part of the subtle body closest to the physical level, emanating about an inch from the body, is the *etheric* or *vital* body. This is most interesting because it vibrates at a frequency which can be detected by a high voltage technique called Kirlian photography. The information captured by this process shows a kind of luminescence and streams of energy flowing from the hands or feet. To the trained eye, these patterns reflect the emotional and physical state of the individual and can be used as a diagnostic tool.

A healthy aura is rather like a filter, allowing only that which is beneficial to affect us. The Bach Flower Remedies seek to harmonize the subtle energy frequencies within the aura which can become weakened by the stresses and strains of life. A weakened aura will give rise to illness. In order to enhance the action of the Remedies, we can learn to control and strengthen our own aura. This is an excellent discipline because a strong aura protects us from influences of all kinds – anything from germs to stress (see Chapter 7).

IN HIS OWN WORDS

Let us conclude this chapter with a few quotations gleaned from Bach's concise work entitled *Heal Thyself*.[5]

Disease will never be cured or eradicated by present materialistic methods, for the simple reason that disease in its origin is not material.

The next great principle is the understanding of the Unity of all things: that the Creator of all things is love, and that everything of which we are conscious is in all its infinite number of forms a manifestation of that love.

The Medical School of the future will not particularly interest itself in the ultimate results and products of disease . . . but knowing the true cause of sickness and aware that the obvious physical results are merely secondary, it will concentrate its efforts upon bringing harmony between body, mind and soul which results in the relief of disease.

3

Learning to Prescribe

A S WE HAVE SEEN, the basic principle of Bach Flower Therapy is to 'Treat the patient, not the disease'. Dr Bach believed strongly that physical illness is the result of disharmony between mind and spirit. In psychotherapy the spirit is often called the 'higher self' – the all-wise aspect that manifests itself in those rare and precious moments of inspiration and clarity; those moments of profound insight into the real purpose of our existence.

The higher self is aware of our true mission in life and endeavours to realize this through the mind and emotions: the personality. However, the personality is not always aware of the higher self, so we often fail to hear the promptings of our inner voice. We go through life only half awake, guided by social conditioning and our subjective responses to the life experience. As a result, according to Bach, instead of experiencing joyfulness, purposefulness, wisdom, and courage, we experience disharmony. If we could act wholly in harmony with our own spirit or higher self (which itself is a part of the greater whole, embracing the rest of humanity, the planet, and the Cosmos), we would fulfil our potential and experience profound happiness. Where there is a disconnection between the higher self and the personality, there is dis-ease.

The ultimate healing potential of the Flower Remedies stems from their ability to release the energy block between the personality and the higher self. In this way, the Remedies help to bring about the necessary change in outlook, without which there can be no true healing.

Of course, the physical body is an interrelated part of the whole

17

– the body-mind-spirit. Therefore, it is important to become aware of our needs on every level. We cannot neglect the body in favour of attaining spiritual awareness, nor pursue the path of physical/material gratification at the expense of our spiritual needs. The result would be an imbalance of energies.

Surely though, some disorders are purely physical in origin – food poisoning, malaria, typhoid, and so on? The answer must be yes and no depending on one's perspective. As far as we on the Earthly plane of awareness are concerned, disease can stem from this level and filter through to the more subtle aspects of our being, at least to the emotional and mental levels. However, according to esoteric philosophy (which mirrors Bach's own beliefs), life on Earth is a schooling. The spiritual aspect has chosen to learn and grow through illness, suffering and setback, even through congenital defect, mental illness and poverty. So in this sense, the true origin of illness and suffering (even accidents) is spiritual. Life was never meant to be easy – and that is the hardest lesson of all to learn. Unfortunately, it is beyond the scope of this little book to go deeply into the whys and wherefores of esoteric philosophy. So I urge the enquiring reader to obtain a copy of Edward Bach's *Heal Thyself*.

PRESCRIBING FOR ONESELF

Self-knowledge

Before we can begin to prescribe for others, we need to achieve self-knowledge. If you are a therapist or are otherwise involved with the 'growth movement', then you will be aware of the importance of self-knowledge as a prerequisite for understanding others. However, the most difficult feat in the quest is to be able to look at another person without being blinkered by one's own hang-ups, life experiences, social conditioning, religious persuasion, and prejudices. Very few human beings actually reach such a non-judgmental position, but we can at least try. We can begin by becoming conscious of our own stumbling blocks, conditioning, and areas of restricted growth. That is the first step. The second step is to work with the Flower Remedies.

Observe how you feel when you need a particular Remedy, and how you feel after taking it. If your life is on an even keel at present, then it will of course, be difficult to gauge any significant change in outlook. However, few of us are totally free from inner conflict, so you could try prescribing the Remedies according to your dreams. The subconscious never forgets unresolved conflict, even though the conscious mind often does (see Dreamwork page 21).

A common difficulty in self-diagnosis, especially when one is going through a crisis, is the inability to step back from oneself sufficiently to be able to recognize which Flowers are required. This is where a friend or a Bach Flower practitioner can help. Talking things through with an understanding person who can empathize with us is a necessary part of the healing process and can help us connect with our own inner strength.

Responses to Treatment

During the first weeks of treatment, the Flower radiations may only embrace the superficial emotions rather than the deep-rooted fears and conflicts which are causing the present physical and mental condition. However, by dealing with each new emotional state as it arises, earlier blockages will eventually work through to the surface and out of your system. When this happens you might notice a temporary worsening of physical symptoms, and experience lesser or greater crises of consciousness. Any aggravation will only last a few days and should be taken as a positive sign that the correct Remedy has been chosen. It is often said that 'one cannot get out what is not already there', so such a reaction is not a side effect, as in drug therapy, but an indication that your own bodymind is correcting itself, the Flower Remedies acting as a catalyst in the process.

It should be emphasized that the intensity of the reaction appears to relate to individual sensitivity and to one's basic openness to change. The majority of people notice subtle changes over a period of weeks or months, gradually feeling more optimistic and better able to deal with the ups and downs of life.

However, should you feel overwhelmed by the changes taking place within your body and mind, though this is a rare occurrence, you should discontinue use of the Flower Remedies and seek professional help from a Bach therapist or counsellor well-versed in the area of 'personal growth'.

Finding the Right Remedy

On first acquaintance with the Flower Remedy descriptions in Chapter 5, you may feel you need all of them! Bach made a point of testing out a composite of all thirty-eight Remedies, but was not satisfied with the result. He found the vibration of one correctly chosen Flower had a deeper and more profound effect than several. However, many people may temporarily require a composite of six or more Flowers.

The best way to begin is to write down the Remedies you feel you need, then look at each one more closely in order to ascertain which is your basic Type Remedy and which are the Helpers.

Type Remedies   The Type Remedy is the Flower vibration that corresponds to your basic character as a whole. You may be an extrovert, a natural leader, and very outspoken. This would suggest Remedies such as **Vine**, **Vervain** and **Impatiens**. If on the other hand you are quiet and reserved, then look to Remedies such as **Mimulus**, **Centaury** or **Water Violet**. Of course, each Flower vibration has its positive as well as its negative aspect. The positive side to the **Impatiens** type, for instance, is seen in those who, though quick to learn, are patient and understanding of those who are not as bright. However, when the vibrations of the **Impatiens** type slow down, the negative aspect of this personality comes to the fore: impatience and lack of tact with those who are not as quick on the uptake. One's Type Remedy might therefore be needed at intervals over the course of one's life.

Helper Remedies   The Helper Remedies address the superficial emotional states of mind that are not characteristic, but are temporary. For instance, you may harbour feelings of jealousy or hatred towards a former partner's new lover (**Holly**), or feel nervous and apprehensive before a court case (**Mimulus**).

Interestingly, Bach observed that the way a person behaves when unwell is often the key to their Type Remedy. On the whole, most of the thirty-eight Remedies can act as either a Type Remedy or a Helper Remedy.

Learning how to select Remedies   It should not be too difficult to limit your choice to within six Remedies, but if you feel you need seven or eight, it is better to include them all than unintentionally to omit one of the essential Flowers. In time, experience will help you refine the process of selection.

The following tried and tested methods will aid familiarization with the Flower Remedies:

1. Try to 'prescribe' for characters in television soaps or in novels. Fictional characters are usually exaggerated versions of real people, and so display quite definite personality traits. Or, to make it slightly more difficult, practise diagnosing Type Remedies for people in the public eye – politicians, members of the Royal Family or TV personalities, for example. Observe your own family, friends and neighbours.
2. Look back over your life and identify the emotional states that predominated at different stages. How did you feel on your first day at school, for instance? Were you happy and self-assured, the dominant child within the group (**Vine**)? Or did you feel intimidated by the exuberance of the other children and therefore too shy to join in? (**Mimulus**). What about your love life? Were you always the rejected partner, the over-possessive lover who stifled the joy and spontaneity out of every relationship (**Chicory**)? Or have you always been the victim, the willing slave to a stronger, more forceful personality (**Centaury**)?
3. Now think of the present. Consider how you respond to criticism; how you might react if you were short-changed at the supermarket; how you deal with illness and pain. By observing your reactions to the life experience, you will soon determine the correct Type Remedy.

Dreamwork

Though not a traditional way of working with the Flower Remedies, in my own experience basic Dreamwork is an invaluable tool in Bach therapy. It is a method which can be employed in self-diagnosis and, when you have gained experience, in the diagnosis of others.

Most dreams represent situations and patterns needing resolution and, contrary to what you may believe, dreams do not generally provide answers to our problems (though they have been known to do so). Instead, they pose questions and invite responses. Therefore, rather than getting bogged down in dream symbolism and interpretation, which can be very misleading to the beginner, concentrate on the feelings and responses, or lack of response, your dreams evoke in you, and prescribe accordingly. For example, you may be shocked by an expression of jealousy and violence in a dream (**Holly**), or by some other equally powerful reaction rarely expressed in the non-dreaming state. It is a fact that what we do not deal with in life will come up in our dreams – recurring dreams are particularly significant in this respect. Likewise, the inability to sleep is sometimes due to a resistance to process repressed material requiring expression.

Interestingly, if your dream reactions are similar to those in your outer life, then this indicates that you have already achieved a certain amount of self-awareness. If they are very different, however, then this suggests there is much repressed emotion to be dealt with. Equally if you are an observer in the dream world, the chances are that you are also an observer in life.

The Flower Remedies tend to activate the dream life which is why it is useful to keep a record of your dreams for about a month whilst taking the Remedies (prescribed in the normal manner). Once you can identify recurring themes and emotions, you will be in a good position to begin deeper work with the Remedies. In fact, you can even ask for a significant dream just before falling asleep; the sub-conscious will usually oblige.

Keep a pen and notebook beside the bed, and immediately on waking (for dreams fade very quickly) write down all you can remember about a significant dream (there is no need to record every dream). If the memory of a dream does evade you, record the particular emotion or mood it may have evoked. Then, try to answer the following questions which are based on the work of dream therapist Strephon Kaplan-Williams. Do not be concerned if you cannot answer every question fully; simply deal with as many issues as you can. The purpose of the exercise is to enable you to view your dreams from the Bach Therapy perspective:

1. What am I doing and why am I doing it?
2. What do I most need to deal with in this dream?
3. Would I react this way in life, or am I reacting in a very different way?
4. What in this dream is related to things in other dreams I have had?
5. What in this dream is related to what is going on in me or in my life at present?
6. Why did I have this dream? What am I needing to look at, or make a choice about?

Consider the following dream recorded by Sarah, a woman in her early forties just on the brink of a new career in psychiatric nursing. She had chosen to work with the Remedies as a means to self-knowledge. Interestingly, Sarah had been taking **Larch** for lack of confidence. Shortly before falling asleep one night she asked her higher self for a dream that would give her further insight into her problems. Her request was duly granted:

> I had just given birth to an unwanted baby. I put the beautiful smiling infant into a carry-cot which I shoved on top of the wardrobe out of the way. The midwife came to examine me, but I felt dirty and embarrassed because I had not washed since giving birth. But the stronger emotion of guilt spurred me into action. I ran ahead of the midwife into the bedroom where I pulled down the carry-cot just in the nick of time! I breathed a sigh of relief; my guilty secret had not been rumbled.

Now, a psychoanalyst would have a field day with this dream! However, in Bach Therapy the most important aspects of the dream are the dreamer's feelings and actions or *reactions*. The Flower Remedies will do the rest – that is to say, they will trigger the process of healing by addressing the feelings of guilt and uncleanliness, which incidentally stem from Sarah's very strict, sexually repressed childhood. The Flower Remedies chosen in this instance were **Crab Apple**, for self-disgust and a need to be cleansed, and **Pine** for guilt.

As a final word on dreams, in my own experience the Bach Remedies seem to envelop one in a protective bubble so that potentially terrifying dreams do not cause undue distress. It is as if the Remedies come equipped with a psychic safety catch!

PRESCRIBING FOR OTHERS

Once you have worked with the Remedies for a while and can prescribe for yourself, you should be able to prescribe for your family and friends. In fact, some Bach Flower users have said that self-diagnosis is sometimes more difficult than diagnosing for those whom we know well. This is because when one's spirits are low it is not easy to be totally objective about oneself. However, diagnosing for a complete stranger requires a little more skill, so let us begin at that level.

The Consultation

A good therapist is a person who has developed two essential skills: the ability to empathize and the capacity to listen.

To empathize is not only to put ourselves in another's place, it is also to be able to connect both with our own and with the other person's inner strength. In so doing, we help to lift them from their negativity, *without becoming engulfed by their suffering*. It is vital to recognize the difference between empathy and sympathy. The feeling of *empathy* is closely linked with our intuitive self, whereas *sympathy* hooks into our personal distress, thereby draining our emotional energy. So prior to the consultation you will find it helpful to spend a few minutes concentrating on becoming centred and connected with your higher self (see page 109).

To listen as a therapist is to hear on various levels. We listen with the intellect to the words they use and the way their story is expressed. For instance: 'I've tried everything, but what's the use' (**Gorse**). Or: 'I know it's all my fault, I should have been more understanding' (**Pine**). Do they speak in a low and anxious voice (**Mimulus**)? Or do they lean forward, clasp your arm and swamp you with their life story – including a graphic account of all their illnesses (**Heather**)?

We should also listen with our eyes, observing their body language. Are they relaxed and self-assured, sitting back comfortably in the chair? Or are they perched on the edge, drumming their fingers on the table?

Above all, we should listen with our intuition – our higher self. It is by being connected with this loving source that we are able to hear between the actual words. Perhaps there is something in their eyes that speaks of grief, anger, bitterness, or fear – even though at this stage they may not have acknowledged the harbouring of such feelings.

If the person finds it difficult to express their emotional outlook, gently guide them in the right direction by asking about their childhood, occupation, home life, and so forth. Try to establish how they react to the life experience. For instance, if they mention bereavement, divorce, or a broken love affair, try to discover how they coped at the time. Did they resort to alcohol, overeating, undereating, drugs (including prescribed tranquillizers and anti-depressants as well as so-called recreational drugs)? What situations do they fear at present: an imminent operation, childbirth, a change of job, a move to another country, retirement?

Sometimes the effects of shock can be so delayed that years might pass before any sign becomes apparent – perhaps in the guise of depression, guilt, or fear. The trauma of abortion, a car crash, or the death of a loved one may lie at the root of a person's present physical and emotional state. In such circumstances always prescribe **Star Of Bethlehem** for the shock, and other Remedies to help the depression, fear, guilt, or whatever it might be.

Interestingly, Dr Bach observed that whenever a person appears to need many Remedies, or if they do not respond to treatment, **Holly** or **Wild Oat** may be the catalyst needed. The vibration of either Flower will 'open' a case, bringing to the surface the predominant underlying emotions. As a result, it should then be much easier to prescribe appropriately. Give **Holly** when the person is of an active or intense nature, and **Wild Oat** when they are more passive.

In chronic conditions such as arthritis and eczema, Dreamwork may reveal which unpleasant feelings lie at the root of the illness. The Flower Remedies, by embracing the repressed emotions, will then trigger the process of true healing; but it is important for the person to co-operate on every level by seeking an appropriate physical therapy such as herbal medicine or chiropractic manipulation, and to find out as much as they can about diet in relation to their illness.

As the person talks, jot down all the Remedies that come to mind. However, try not to let note-taking become too obtrusive. It is important to maintain a relaxed and equal relationship, an atmosphere of trust, throughout the consultation. You can always make notes immediately afterwards while the person's story is still fresh in your mind.

When discussing the Flower Remedies with the person always dwell on the positive qualities or virtues to be achieved by them. For instance, instead of emphasizing that **Gentian** is for their 'doubting Thomas' attitude, let them go away with the knowledge that **Gentian** will help them develop the certainty that their problems can be overcome.

My own approach is usually to include some 'homework' such as breathing exercises, a relaxation tape, visualization, or slow stretching movements to release physical and emotional tension. If there is a great deal of self-disgust I suggest ways of nurturing the self. This might include a daily aromatic bath with a few drops of **Crab Apple** added to the aromatherapy oils; or something simple such as buying themselves a small present once in a while – a few fresh flowers, a tiny crystal, an exotic fruit, a beautiful picture card, and so on.

Finally, the most difficult thing for any therapist to accept is that a person might not be ready to let go of their illness, albeit on a subconscious level. This should not be seen as a failure on anyone's part. The origin of their suffering may be *karmic*, which means on one level that their spirit has chosen the illness as an experience essential to its development. Nora Weeks, a long-time colleague of Dr Bach, would say of those who took the Remedies prior to passing on: 'Well they at least died happy!'

SPECIAL USES FOR FLOWER REMEDIES

Pregnancy

The beautiful vibrations of the Flower Remedies are perfectly safe and highly beneficial to the expectant mother and her unborn child. The method of diagnosis and treatment is no different from usual. The Remedies can be of help where there is apprehension or emotional suffering during the pre- and post-natal periods. Many practitioners suggest a basic composite of **Rescue Remedy** and **Walnut**. This mixture can be taken a few days before the expected date of delivery, during labour, and for about a month afterwards to help both mother and child cope with reaction and change.

Incidentally, there are many recorded cases of mothers having experienced an easy and gentle birth and a rapid recovery as a result of taking **Rescue Remedy** shortly before parturition.[6]

In addition to the aforementioned Remedies, others can be added or replaced accordingly. For example: **Mimulus** for fear of childbirth (or in extreme cases, **Rock Rose**); and **Impatiens** to help those who become irritable and impatient as they near term – a common state of mind, especially when the baby is overdue. During labour other Remedies such as **Oak**, **Hornbeam**, and **Olive** may be indicated if the woman is exhausted and feels she can no longer carry on; and during the post-natal period **Mustard, Gorse, Gentian, Sweet Chestnut** or **Willow** may have a role to play in uplifting the spirits of the mother suffering from 'baby blues'.

Babies

You might be surprised to learn that newborn babies are relatively easy to diagnose, even though they are unable to tell us about their state of mind. For example: the **Agrimony** baby is usually happy and gurgling and is very little trouble – unless there is something definitely wrong; the **Chicory** baby is very demanding, always wanting attention, and hating to be alone; the **Clematis** baby on the other hand shows very little interest in anything, sleeping a great deal and sometimes having to be woken up for his feeds; the **Mimulus** baby is very nervous, frightened by loud noises and sudden movements; while the **Impatiens** baby has quite a little temper!

Bach believed that by addressing the baby's type or personality difficulty, the passing moods or negative states of mind would be easily transmuted, before they began to take root. When a spirit can be helped at this stage, its passage through life will be much easier and happier for the personality. What a wonderful thought! The dosage is the same as for adults, though nursing mothers can take the Remedy themselves (see page 88).

Children

Children (and animals too) are a joy for the Bach Flower practitioner for they often respond rapidly and extremely well to the Remedies. This is because the child tends to express his or her feelings openly – that is, until the self-conscious phase of adolescence. Adults, of course, are not only conditioned by society, but also by their own habitual responses to the ups and downs of life, particularly the downs. The pattern of distress then becomes deeply ingrained, and thus more difficult to transmute.

First, try to establish the child's Type Remedy if you can. This will be required at intervals throughout childhood, and indeed into maturity, unless the personality changes radically (not an unknown phenomenon). Then establish which other Remedies will be supportive. For example: **Walnut**, the Remedy for change or transition, is most helpful during the turbulence of puberty. **Vine** will help transmute the aggressive energy of the school bully into positive qualities of leadership. **Centaury** on the other hand will help the bully's victim! **Holly** will embrace the child who is jealous of her baby brother, while **Rock Rose** or **Rescue Remedy** will dispel her nightmares. If the child's disturbing dreams are caused by a recurrent upsetting memory, then **Honeysuckle** is indicated. For fear of the dark, consider **Mimulus**; for vague fears of unknown origin, especially if accompanied by sweating and trembling, turn to **Aspen**; for the wakeful, highly active child choose **Vervain**; and for the drowsy, apathetic child prescribe **Clematis**. Finally, not forgetting the long-suffering, over-anxious parent, **Red Chestnut** will engender a sense of calm and positivity.

Animals

As verified by numerous veterinary case studies,[7] animals tend to respond to the Flower Remedies even more rapidly, and sometimes more profoundly, than humans. The diagnosis is made in the usual way, though one must try to empathize with the animal in order to perceive its state of mind. The nervous animal, for instance, who tends to jump with fright at the slightest sound or any sudden movement needs **Mimulus**. The over-possessive dog who drives his owner berserk by being constantly at her heels could do with a dose of **Chicory**. The jealous, suspicious dog who barks at everyone needs **Holly**. The cat with nine lives who has been hit by a car on more than one occasion needs **Chestnut Bud** to enable it to learn from past mistakes, and so on.

George MacLeod, one of the world's foremost authorities on the use of homoeopathic remedies for animals, encourages all his fellow vets to use the **Rescue Remedy** for shock, accidents, injuries, pre-surgical work, and so forth. 'Dr Bach was a medical genius', he says.

Plants

Yes, even plants can respond to the Flower Remedies, for example when suffering from pest damage or when being transplanted. **Rescue Remedy** is indispensable in this respect, followed by **Walnut** and **Crab Apple** (see Chapter 5).

4

The Thirty-Eight Healers

D R BACH GROUPED the Remedies under seven headings:

1. For those who have fear: **Rock Rose, Mimulus, Cherry Plum, Aspen, Red Chestnut.**
2. For those who suffer uncertainty: **Cerato, Scleranthus, Gentian, Gorse, Hornbeam, Wild Oat.**
3. For insufficient interest in present circumstances: **Clematis, Honeysuckle, Wild Rose, Olive, White Chestnut, Mustard, Chestnut Bud.**
4. For loneliness: **Water Violet, Impatiens, Heather.**
5. For those over-sensitive to influences and ideas: **Agrimony, Centaury, Walnut, Holly.**
6. For despondency and despair: **Larch, Pine, Elm, Sweet Chestnut, Star of Bethlehem, Willow, Oak, Crab Apple.**
7. For over-care for the welfare of others: **Chicory, Vervain, Vine, Beech, Rock Water.**

For easy reference, the Flower Remedies appear in this chapter in alphabetical order. Each Remedy profile is presented as follows:

  Line drawing and botanical note
  Method of potentization
  Key negative state of mind
  A more detailed description of the negative state
  Positive potential following treatment
  Other self-help measures
  The child for whom the Remedy is indicated

The first two points are self-explanatory, so let us consider the key negative state of a mind. This is a summary to facilitate immediate diagnosis. A more detailed account follows to confirm whether or not you have chosen the correct Remedy. However, a person does not have to fit the Remedy description *exactly* as outlined in order for a particular Flower Remedy to be indicated. It is important to have a good knowledge of of the Remedy personalities, spiced with a little intuition. With practice, it will soon become second nature to perceive the 'atmosphere' of a person and to prescribe accordingly.

The positive potential following treatment is, of course, the ultimate transmutation whereby the positive aspects within the psyche are brought to the fore, freed from the chains of fear, doubt, anger, and uncertainty. It would be unrealistic, however, to suggest that the Bach Remedies alone can bring about such a remarkable change in every case, especially if the condition is very deep-rooted. Therefore, it is important when treating yourself or others to recognize your own or the other person's limitations and to seek professional help where necessary, in the form of counselling, psychotherapy, or even a physical therapy such as massage, herbal medicine, or orthodox treatment. As we have seen, the Remedies work in harmony with other treatments, hastening the process of healing.

Other self-help measures such as yoga, positive affirmations, gardening, and so on, are suggested where appropriate because they encourage a full and active participation in our own healing – a very important tenet of holistic therapy. Any of these activities can be practised with, or instead of, Dreamwork (Chapter 3) and the basic relaxation and visualization techniques outlined in Chapter 7. Incidentally, when taking a number of Flower Remedies (as is most common) there is no need to attempt every self-help measure suggested for each Remedy. Just practise whatever you feel would be most helpful.

Sometimes it can be difficult to decide between two Remedies of a similar ilk (the fear Remedies, **Aspen** and **Mimulus**, for example), so where this commonly occurs, a comparison has been drawn to help clarify the matter.

In the case of children, although they may be essentially no different from the adult of a similar disposition, a brief description is included at the end of each section to help further elucidate and round out the picture.

Please note that although the Flower Remedy personalities are described alternately throughout as 'he' or 'she', each Remedy profile of course applies to either sex.

Finally, the **Rescue Remedy** is discussed on page 85. This is a first-aid Remedy combining the following Flowers: **Rock Rose, Clematis, Impatiens, Cherry Plum** and **Star of Bethlehem.**

AGRIMONY
Agrimonia eupatoria

A softly hairy plant with spikes of faintly fragrant yellow flowers. Grows to a height of 30–60 cm. Widespread and common in grassy places. Flowers June–August.

Method of potentization: Sun.

Key negative state: Mental torture concealed behind a happy-go-lucky façade.

The **Agrimony** type is easy to recognize. He is the life and soul of any party: the exuberant yet kindly jester who would never make fun of another, for he laughs only at himself.

So what is wrong with that? you may ask. Nothing at all if it were the whole truth; but **Agrimony** wears the actor's mask of Comedy or Tragedy. The joyful public persona is very different from the creased face of woe that hides in the closet.

Rarely will the true **Agrimony** soul seek help of his own volition. He prefers to go on pretending to the world, and often to himself, that life is just wonderful. When alone (a situation he tries to avoid at all costs) he attempts to stifle the worrying thoughts that bombard his consciousness, but with very little success. Often he has trouble sleeping and may even resort to alcohol or drugs as an escape from his problems.

Only the one he loves and trusts the most will ever be allowed to glimpse the truth – and it is this person who will encourage and, with luck, eventually persuade him to seek the help he so desperately needs.

Positive potential following treatment: The ability *truly* to laugh at life because personal problems will be viewed from a more balanced perspective – that of the genuine optimist who possesses an innate talent for creating harmony where there is discord.

Other self-help measures: Join a relaxation, yoga, or Tai Chi class – or obtain a relaxation tape.

Where there is a drink or drugs related problem, seek expert help. Join Alcoholics Anonymous or a self-help group geared to overcoming drug addiction. Incidentally, these groups are not solely for people hooked on so-called recreational drugs; they also offer support for those addicted to prescribed drugs such as Valium.

Where to find information: Check the advertisements in local newspapers, or the notice-boards in doctors' waiting-rooms, clinics, and public libraries. Your local telephone directory may also be a source of contacts.

The Agrimony child: This child appears outwardly cheerful but, as his mother or closest carer knows, he suffers inwardly. Great importance is attached to the impression he is making on his friends, family and teachers.

ASPEN
Populus tremula

A small tree, up to about 15m, related to the great black poplar. Found throughout Britain on poor soils and in damp woodland. Flowers February–April.

Method of potentization: Boiling.

Key negative state: Inexplicable fears stemming from the psyche; nightmares; fear of some impending evil.

Comparison: Compare with **Mimulus** whose fear is of *known* or worldly origin (fear of an impending court case, for example).

The **Aspen** type, like the delicate tree itself, trembles in the slightest breeze. She is hypersensitive to 'bad vibes' of any nature, be it the eerie atmosphere of a building or the unpleasant undertones sometimes generated within groups of people. She will also be disturbed by the 'sinister shadows' surrounding certain individuals whom she suspects of being mentally unbalanced in some way; or she may awaken in the night, trembling and sweating, terrified by the notion that something evil lurks behind the wardrobe.

Although it is said that **Aspen**'s fears are of the mind, this does not necessarily mean that they are a fantasy. She may be very psychic but, instead of tuning into the joyous events of life, she tends to focus on catastrophe: an impending plane crash or a bomb explosion, for instance.

Positive potential following treatment: Fearlessness in the knowledge that one's Guardian is the universal power of Love.

Other self-help measures: Try auric control (see page 108). Regular practice of this technique will not act to diminish any genuine psychic ability but will serve as a mode of psychic protection, a filter against harmful thoughts and influences of any nature. Most importantly, it will allow much more control over what comes through.

Choose activities which are 'grounding' such as gardening,

walking, sport, cooking, receiving or giving massage – or even watching a funny film or play.

Avoid anything that will disturb the mind, such as horror films or books, and intoxicants such as alcohol or cannabis. It may also be wise to avoid any conscious form of psychic development such as occult practice or even yoga, unless under the guidance of an experienced tutor.

The Aspen child: This child suffers from recurring nightmares and may even sleepwalk. Very often demands that a light be left on all night.

BEECH
Fagus sylvatica

A majestic tree widespread throughout Britain, growing to a height of 30–40m. The male and female flowers appear on the same plant forming a purplish brown tassle on a long stalk. Blooms April–May.

Method of potentization: Boiling.

Key negative state: Intolerance, criticism and arrogance.

Comparisons: Compare with **Vine** whose need is to dominate, and with **Vervain**, the forceful fanatic whose need is to convert.

The **Beech** personality perceives little that is good or beautiful in the world. He has few friends because his hypercritical and intolerant nature irritates others beyond measure. He sees no virtue in the diversity of human nature, his motto being: 'Why can't they do as I do?'

Beech often fails to recognize the fact that not everyone is born with the same gifts or has the same social or cultural background. Even the small habits, gestures, and mannerisms of others are annoying, the degree of displeasure bearing no relation to the cause.

Sadly, his own life may have been one of hard-swallowed hatred, humiliation, and disappointment. This bitterness, which often manifests as digestive upsets, is projected on to the outside world, for **Beech** has yet to reach his innermost feelings. As a result of this suppression, he finds it impossible to enter into the feelings of others.

Positive potential following treatment: Tolerance and understanding of the difficulties of others; the ability to see the good in everyone and everything.

Other self-help measures: When criticizing others, notice whether they are generalized criticisms such as 'He's stupid' or 'She's a bore'. If so, change generalized criticism to specific descriptions of behaviour so that 'She's a fool' becomes 'She giggles when nervous' or 'She's too loud', for example. Then begin to look for the positive qualities in people. How do they relate to their children, neighbours, workmates, and so forth? List their skills and abilities. The act of consciously looking for positive traits in other's, and writing them down to remind yourself, counteracts the tendency to see everything and everyone in negative terms.

Commune with nature as often as possible.

Take up some form of physical activity which counteracts rigidity of body and mind, such as dancing, yoga, Tai Chi, and so on. Seek some frivolity in life!

The Beech child: He may be reflecting parental attitudes (consider this deeply), or perhaps he is feeling belittled by an elder, more dominant or popular sibling.

CENTAURY
Centaurium erythraea

A variable annual, 5–35cm tall (depending on habitat). Widespread and common in poor, dry, grassy places and on dunes. The

small rose-pink, star-like flowers open only in bright sunshine. Blooms June–August.

Method of potentization: Sun.

Key negative state: Lack of will-power to refuse the demands of others, therefore becoming a willing slave.

Centaury believes she was born to serve. She suppresses her own needs simply to keep the peace and to gain favour in the eyes of another. The **Vine** or **Vervain** type will spot her immediately!

Centaury may even forgo marriage and a family of her own in order to care for an ageing parent or relative. Often she is tired, sometimes completely drained by the incessant demands of other people, yet she rarely complains for she is resigned to drudgery.

Sadly, **Centaury** misses out on many things in life, particularly the joy and excitement that independence and a sense of adventure often bring.

Should she marry, the chances are that she will attract a tyrant. But why does she choose such a doormat existence? It has been said that **Centaury** connects with a stronger personality in order to evade the process of growing up which would involve making her own decisions. Therefore, like a child, **Centaury** unconsciously submits to a strong and forceful person because she cannot connect with her own inner strength.

Positive potential following treatment: To know when to give and when to withhold: the ability to mix with others while preserving one's own identity; to live life according to one's own true mission.

Other self-help measures: Take up a martial art such as judo which will help to cultivate inner strength, poise and self-confidence; attend a class in assertiveness training.

Practise the aura strengthening visualization (see page 108).

The Centaury child: She is quiet, sensitive, responsive – hardly any trouble, but she may be the prey of the school bully.

CERATO
Ceratostigma willmottiana

The only cultivated plant used in the Bach system, **Cerato** is a flowering shrub from the Himalayas, about 60cm in height. The beautiful bright blue flowers open in August and September.

Method of potentization: Sun.

Key negative state: Insufficient confidence in themselves to make their own decisions.

Comparison: **Scleranthus** is torn between two things, but unlike **Cerato**, rarely bothers others with the trivia of day to day decision-making. **Scleranthus** eventually struggles to find the answer from within.

Cerato is plagued with uncertainty. Even though he is intuitive and possesses sound judgement, he rarely trusts the promptings of his inner voice, and thus cannot act on his own volition. Instead, he drives his family and friends to distraction with his incessant demands for advice or confirmation of the wisdom of his every action.

Not only is **Cerato** easily swayed by the opinions of others, but he has also been known to imitate the style of dress and even the gestures and mannerisms of the one he most admires which can, of course, make him appear foolish at times.

He will experience the occasional moment of clarity in which he will pour out his most frequent lament, 'I *knew* I should have done that. Now it's too late!' Or, having drained the energy of just about everyone in his vicinity, he will infuriatingly decide to do it his own way after all!

Positive potential following treatment: To trust one's own ability to judge between right and wrong; to act and remain uninfluenced by any advice to the contrary.

Other self-help measures: Try visualization: using the basic technique described in Chapter 7, concentrate on the idea of making contact with your higher self. Then, in your mind's eye, see yourself making an important decision and acting on it. Know that the outcome will be favourable and feel good about it. Regular practice of this visualization will enable you eventually to realize your objective.

Dreamwork can also be useful (see Chapter 3).

The Cerato child: This state of mind is more likely to emerge during adolescence. **Cerato** constantly seeks the approval of others (particularly his peers) and insists on wearing the most fashionable clothes, whether they suit him or not! It may be wise to let the young person grow out of this phase in his own good time (a valuable learning experience). However, if he is attached to a truly 'bad crowd' then **Cerato** combined with **Walnut** will help him to sever the links.

CHERRY PLUM
Prunus cerasifera

A small thornless tree growing to a height of 6–8m. The flowers are pure white, slightly larger than those of the Sloe (*P. spinosa*) with which it is sometimes confused. Common as a hedgerow shrub, mainly in the south of England. Flowers from late February to early April.

Method of potentization: Boiling.

Key negative state: Fear of losing one's mind; uncontrolled outbreaks of temper.

Cherry Plum harbours a morbid fear that she lives on borrowed time. She feels that at any moment she may lose her grip on reality – the bottomless pit of insanity gapes before her.

There is also the terrible impulse to harm other people or herself. Thoughts of suicide wash in and out of her mind like some menacing black tide.

But how did she reach such a state of desperation? She may have suffered a prolonged period of anxiety or grief and now finds herself on the verge of a nervous breakdown. Or for many years she may have dealt with the trials and tribulations of life in an outwardly controlled and 'dignified' manner. But the turbulence of unexpressed emotion causes great pressure and distortion; destructive images and forces eventually thrust their way to the surface. **Cherry Plum** is no longer able to hold back, and the volcano erupts! However, with the right kind of emotional support, no serious damage will ensue, for the volcano is her psychic safety valve.

Cherry Plum is included in the **Rescue Remedy** for violent outbursts and hysteria (see page 85).

Positive potential following treatment: The ability to handle great inner forces spontaneously and with a true sense of calm, for the distress is healed by the balancing forces of the spirit or higher self.

Other self-help measures: If feeling suicidal, do seek expert help – phone the Samaritans and/or contact your doctor. Find out about psychotherapy, especially if **Cherry Plum** is your Type Remedy.

Instead of turning aggressive energy inwards, learn to harness it, using its dynamism to give more steam to any project or activity: only get in touch with the powerful energy when you are actually feeling some form of aggression. That is to say, feel its vigour, its vibrancy, the effect it has on your body. Now realize that these feelings are at your disposal – know that, although they can hurt, they can also become the propelling force for any activity you have chosen. It may be a blitz on the housework, or a long overdue letter of complaint to the local council – or why not start that novel?

The Cherry Plum child: There may be sudden uncontrolled outbreaks of rage, especially when the child throws herself on the ground or hits her head against the wall – the typical temper tantrum.

CHESTNUT BUD
Aesculus hippocastanum

The Horse Chestnut tree was brought to Britain from Turkey in the early seventeenth century. Only the sticky buds are used for this Remedy, the flowers being used for **White Chestnut** essence. The buds are picked in early April.

Method of potentization: Boiling.

Key negative state: Failure to learn by experience; need for repetition.

Chestnut Bud experiences *déjà vu* more than most. But instead of being a rather pleasant or intriguing experience, it tends to lead to that same old feeling, 'Oh no, not again!' Over and over again he makes the same mistakes, failing to learn from others or from past experiences. Indeed, by obsessively blocking out the past he is rather like a house built without foundations, certain to collapse in a strong wind.

Why does **Chestnut Bud** constantly come up against the same stumbling blocks? The reason may be indifference, too much haste, or lack of observation. In a sense, he is a young spirit flowing against the tide of life. In his naivety, he fails to learn life's most fundamental lesson: that we cannot escape from the past into the future, for the future reflects the past, even though our real development is taking place in the present, in the eternal NOW.

Positive potential following treatment: The ability to keep one's attention in the present; to gain knowledge and wisdom from every experience.

Other self-help measures: In a state of deep relaxation (see Chapter 7), or just before falling asleep, ask yourself: Why do I keep hitting the same barrier? What am I supposed to be learning from this experience? Then ask: What changes do I need to make in order to progress? Practise this daily until you receive insight.

The answers may come in various ways and through different channels: perhaps in a moment of inspiration during or immediately after the exercise. Or the message might come more slowly and in a subtle way, so that after a while you realize that your outlook has become clear even though the actual moment of insight cannot be pin-pointed. The answers may even reach you through a dream or, more curiously, through *synchronicity*; that is to say, through some element in the environment that you perceive as meaningful. It could be a phrase read at random in a book, an event that changes your usual routine, the title of a film, or the words of a friend, and so on. Indeed, the answer may be 'blowing in the wind' – if you are able to catch it!

The Chestnut Bud child: This child finds it difficult to pay attention; he is a slow learner. In spite of being reminded, he will keep forgetting his P.E. kit or his pencil case, for instance.

CHICORY
Cichorium intybus

A perennial herb up to 1m in height, common on chalky soil. Grows on wasteland and on the edges of fields and roadsides. The pretty blue flowers open in July to September, but last only a day, fading as soon as they are picked.

Method of potentization: Sun.

Key negative state: Possessiveness; self-pity.

Chicory cannot express unconditional love, for the love aspect is hindered in its outward flow, and is turned inward to the self. **Chicory** demands sympathy and appreciation from others, yet rarely can she give as much in return, or if she does, there is always a price to pay: 'I love you on condition that . . .'

If she does not receive the love and affection she believes is her due, she will become manipulative and deceitful, engendering a sense of guilt in those susceptible to emotional blackmail.

As a parent, **Chicory** is inclined to be possessive and over-protective, causing her children to feel stifled by such an engulfing embrace. She is compelled to control and direct – organizing, criticizing, and generally frog-marching her loved ones through life. And of course, she suffers deep resentment when they later rebel.

Sadly, **Chicory** may have had a childhood devoid of love. She feels a deep inner emptiness and lack of fulfilment, so craves recognition and affection. But her need is as vast as a bottomless pit that can never be filled.

Positive potential following treatment: The ability to give without demanding anything in return; to be secure in oneself.

Other self-help measures: If the problem is deep-rooted rather than a temporary state of mind, it would be helpful to seek counselling, or a nurturing therapy such as aromatherapy (which includes gentle massage).

Commune with nature whenever you can – even your local park could be a source of healing. Find inner peace by practising deep relaxation, breathing and meditation exercises (see Chapter 7).

Begin to change negative thought-patterning by repeating the following affirmation just before you fall asleep at night: 'I am finding security within myself. I allow joy to flow through my mind and body and out to others.'

The Chicory child: This child demands a great deal of attention; she cannot bear to be alone, and may even feign illness to get her own way.

CLEMATIS
Clematis vitalba

A woody climber found in hedgerows and woodland, especially on chalk and limestone soils in the south of Britain and much of Ireland. The trusses of faintly fragrant, greenish-white flowers appear from July to September. The plant is also commonly known as Old Man's Beard because the styles develop into woolly greyish-white plumes in the autumn.

Method of potentization: Sun

Key negative state: Day-dreaming; indifference; little attention in the present; a bemused state of mind; unconsciousness.

Clematis is not of this world. His faraway look and lack of vitality is indicative of one who dwells in the realm of fantasy and dreams. He has little or no interest in the present, for his thoughts are far away in the future, in happier times to come.

It has been said of **Clematis** that he hears without listening and sees without looking, so forgets most of what is said to him. He also likes to sleep, not just at bedtime, but on the bus, at a lecture, in front of the television, in fact almost anywhere and at any time. With his life energies diverted inwards in this way, he never becomes angry or violent, deeply depressed, nor even joyful. Good news is greeted with as much indifference as bad.

In illness **Clematis** makes little or no effort to get better, and may even welcome the prospect of death in the hope of meeting on the spirit plane some beloved one whom he has lost. This extreme lack of effort to get well prompted Bach to call the **Clematis** state of mind 'a polite form of suicide'.

Incidentally, the **Clematis** state may also be of a passing nature, where there is unconsciousness, fainting, or any bemused state of mind brought about by shock. For this reason, **Clematis** is included in the **Rescue Remedy** (see page 85).

Positive potential following treatment: If creative, as most **Clematis** types are, the ability to bring into realization one's creative inspiration. To take a lively interest in all things because the purpose of life can be fully appreciated.

Other self-help measures: Choose activities that are 'grounding' such as gardening, receiving or giving massage, cooking, watching a very funny play or film.

Find an outlet for creativity such as painting, writing, flower arranging, and so on.

Psychic ability may be present, but undisciplined esoteric work of any nature may trigger certain psychological problems, so do seek the advice of a reputable teacher or healer.

The Clematis child: He is pale and sleepy, inattentive and absent-minded. Has a poor body image and tends to bump into things. His eyes are usually unfocused, and he has a dreamy expression.

CRAB APPLE
Malus pumila or *sylvestris*

The true wild apple is a small deciduous tree with a crooked trunk, fissured and cracked. Found in hedgerows, thickets and woodland, and reaching a maximum height of 10m. The clusters of pinkish-white blossom appear in May.

Method of potentization: Boiling.

Key negative state: A feeling of being unclean; self-disgust; over-emphasis on trivial detail.

Crab Apple is filled with a sense of self-disgust. She feels somehow unclean in mind and body. She might have a minor skin blemish such as a pimple on her chin which she examines closely in a magnifying mirror, and then imagines that everyone else can clearly see the pustule in all its hideous magnitude! Or perhaps she has a deep-rooted skin complaint such as eczema or psoriasis which fills her with despair and an overwhelming feeling of self-repugnance. In the same vein, she may be revolted by bodily functions such as breastfeeding, sex, and illness.

Her tendency to home in on detail, to magnify things under the lens of her own limited viewpoint, also spills over into other areas of her life. It may be, for instance, that the puppy has left dirty marks on the freshly washed kitchen floor, but the more important fact that the animal has injured its leg only sinks in once the floor has been re-washed.

Note: **Crab Apple** is also particularly valuable as an external treatment (see pages 89–90).

Positive potential following treatment: The wisdom to see things in their proper perspective; self-respect.

Other self-help measures: Practise the aura strengthening visualization (see Chapter 7).

Indulge in self-nurturing activities such as a daily or weekly aromatic bath containing 5–8 drops of a favourite essential oil e.g. lavender, bergamot, ylang-ylang, lemon, sandalwood. (Essential oils are available from most health shops.) Also add 5 drops of **Crab Apple** to the bath water.

Buy yourself a small present once a day for a week – a few flowers, an appealing picture card, an exotic fruit, and so on.

For very deep-rooted problems manifesting as compulsive washing of the hands, for instance, do seek professional counselling or psychotherapy.

The Crab Apple child: This child is very sensitive; disgusted by such things as insects or worms, eating food from others' plates, or getting dirty. (The child may be reflecting the behaviour of a **Crab Apple** parent.) The Remedy is useful during puberty, for girls who find menstruation distasteful, or for the youngster who is embarrassed by a spotty skin.

ELM
Ulmus procera

Although the ravages of Dutch Elm disease have destroyed most of the mature trees in Britain, many young trees appear to be thriving. A few mature specimens can still be found in some northern counties and in a few isolated nature reserves. Elm flowers are small and reddish brown, appearing in clusters in February and March, before the leaves unfurl.

Method of potentization: Boiling.

Key negative state: Temporary feelings of inadequacy, even though fulfilling one's mission in life.

Comparisons: Compare with **Hornbeam** whose fatigue is through dislike for the work he is doing, while **Olive** is worn out by long and continued stress. The **Elm** exhaustion by contrast is temporary.

The **Elm** person may be succeeding in life, following his own true mission, but occasionally experiences despondency. He suddenly feels he has taken on more responsibility than he can carry, and fears that failure is just around the corner.

He usually holds a position of importance, and is a person upon whom others rely. Indeed, everyone holds him in high esteem, for he is hardworking, capable, and reliable. However, **Elm** is sometimes too altruistic for his own good. He forgets that he has physical and emotional limits. Sudden exhaustion and crisis is the bodymind's cry for rest and moderation in all things. At such times, and indeed as a regular practice, he needs to find a quiet space from which problems can be viewed in perspective, thus restoring his confidence which has been temporarily lost.

Positive potential following treatment: The ability to see problems in their proper perspective; an inner conviction that help will always come at the right moment.

Other self-help measures: Take regular walks in the countryside or in the park; and allow yourself plenty of opportunity for breaks when planning work – including that all-important holiday now and again.

Treat yourself to an aromatherapy massage.

The Elm child: **Elm** is a state of mind not normally associated with young children, though the Remedy may be of use for youngsters suffering from overload at examination time. However, one would need to assess the situation from all angles, finding the right combination of Flower Remedies to suit the young person's individual needs.

GENTIAN
Gentiana amarella (Felwort)

A hairless biennial, 15–20cm in height. Found on dry, chalky or limestone soils, on hills and dunes. The flowers are purple/violet but not blue, nor spotted as in other varieties of Gentian. Blooms only in autumn, from late August to early October.

Method of potentization: Sun.

Key negative state: Being easily discouraged: scepticism – a 'doubting Thomas'.

Comparisons: **Gentian** is the first stage of hopelessness before despondency sets in – the 'two-steps-forward-one-back' feeling. The second stage is **Gorse** when one feels that nothing is going to help us get well. Finally, there is **Sweet Chestnut**, where there is nothing but oblivion ahead, and utter despair.

Like Eeyore, in *Winnie the Pooh*, **Gentian** suffers from a deeply negative outlook. It has been said that 'she wouldn't be happy if she was happy.' She is the eternal pessimist who takes a certain satisfaction in saying 'I told you so.' She fails to see that her own negative outlook actually colours and shapes the course of her life, attracting the very conditions that she dreads the most.

As a temporary state of mind, **Gentian** is for those who suffer a setback during convalescence, for instance, or have doubts about the efficacy of the treatment being given. Their depression is from a known cause, from delay or hindrance – the negativity that breeds a sense of failure.

Positive potential following treatment: To acquire perseverance; the faith of a positive sceptic – one who sees difficulties, but does not fall into a deep gloom over them. The realization that there is no failure when one is doing one's best, whatever the apparent result.

Other self-help measures: Just before you fall asleep at night say the following words: 'There is no failure when I am doing my best.'

The Gentian child: Discouraged by her schoolwork, for instance, she does not want to go back to school; or she may be the child who is torn in two as a result of being dragged back and forth between divorced parents.

GORSE
Ulex europaeus

A spiny evergreen bush or shrub. Widespread in rough grassy places, especially heaths and downs. The bright yellow, almond-scented flowers appear from February onwards, though they are most abundant in April and May.

Method of potentization: Sun.

Key negative state: Hopelessness and despair.

Comparison: Compare with **Wild Rose** who is even more passive and apathetic and is unable to muster the enthusiasm to try again. **Gorse** can be persuaded to try another approach.

The **Gorse** type suffers from the hopelessness of one who has been told 'nothing more can be done to help you'. Believing that fate has decreed suffering as his lot, he makes little mental effort to improve his situation. 'Oh what's the use', he cries, 'I've tried everything humanly possible.' Yet his inner voice of wisdom may still be heard faintly beyond the din of despair. At odd moments he may even glimpse the light shining through the hazy glass partition that separates his personality from its source – the higher self. At such times, unlike **Wild Rose**, he can be persuaded by his loved ones to try again, albeit half-heartedly.

His life's lesson is to open up to the possibility that the higher self is the ferryman of one's destiny; to flow with the tide of life instead of throwing up mental dams, blocking the connection between the personality and the source.

Gorse is also the Remedy for those who have been ill for a long time. It engenders hope, and hope is the first step towards recovery.

Positive potential following treatment: To know that all difficulties will be overcome in the end.

Other self-help measures: Read an uplifting novel, or the biography of one who has overcome horrendous difficulties against all odds.

If your surroundings at home are dull, make every effort to improve the situation. For example, put fresh flowers or potted plants around the house. If possible, re-decorate at least one room in your home with positive and joyful colours such as shades of yellow and gold, peach, clear greens, and pinks.

Create a cheery ambience by vaporizing your favourite essential oils (oils and vaporizers are available from many health or craft shops).

Commune with nature as often as possible.

The Gorse child: The Remedy will help uplift the spirits of the child who may have become despondent as a result of long illness.

HEATHER
Calluna vulgaris

A well-known evergreen shrub, turning huge areas of moorland purple in late summer. Flowers July–September. Blooms are mauve, pink and, occasionally, white.

Method of potentization: Sun.

Key negative state: Self-centredness; fear of loneliness; a poor listener.

'Oh no, it's **Heather**, quick let's hide!' Even caring **Centaury** will feel like dodging **Heather**, for she is a drain on the emotional reserves of just about everyone.

Heather loves to talk – incessantly. She craves an audience and, indeed, has the uncanny knack of steering any conversation towards herself: her love-life, her illnesses, her successes and failures, her psyche, her everything – ad nauseam. No one else can get a word in edgeways! Should you venture to move away, she will move in close, grab your arm, and proceed to suffocate you with an avalanche of exaggerated woe.

Why should **Heather** be so self-centred? It has been said that she is the 'needy child', the lonely adult whose craving for affection and appreciation stems from a childhood starved of such necessities; thus she is unable to take any real interest in the needs of others.

The negative **Heather** state of mind can, of course, be temporary: when we are ill, for example, or going through a crisis such as bereavement, divorce, or some other loss.

Positive potential following treatment: The gift of great empathy as a result of having suffered. To become a good listener. To be secure in oneself.

Other self-help measures: Make every effort to listen to others. Ask questions and wait for a reply.

Practise the aura strengthening visualization in Chapter 7. By strengthening your own energy field, the need to drain the energies of others will be greatly diminished.

The Heather child: She will talk about herself with great exuberance, exaggerating along the way! In fact, the **Heather** state of mind is a natural childhood phase and should never be deemed a problem.

HOLLY
Ilex aquifolium

A small evergreen tree or shrub with glossy, prickly, dark green leaves and red berries. Widespread in woods, hedgerows and thickets. The flowers are small and white, often tinged with purple. Blooms from May to August.

Method of potentization: Boiling.

Key negative state: Envy, jealousy, rage, suspicion, or hatred.

Comparison: Compare with **Willow** who is an introvert, a depressive character who sees herself as a victim. **Holly** is a more active or intense type who can openly express his feelings – at least with those whom he knows well.

The negative **Holly** state is the sub-personality residing within the psyche of each and every one of us. He is King of the Shadow, of envy, jealousy, and spite. By nurturing the roots of hatred, he is the cause of every human difficulty, for hatred is the antithesis of the greatest force of all, that of love.

At times he may lurk beneath the surface, tending the smouldering coals of anger, contempt, and resentment. If the flames of wrath are kept dampened for too long, however, and having no other outlet, they will invade our sleep in the guise of turbulent dreams, until we have no choice but to react with openly expressed venom!

Positive potential following treatment: The ability to give without thought of recompense; to rejoice in the good fortune of others, even when having problems oneself.

Other self-help measures: If the **Holly** state of mind has become chronic, or if much of the negativity smoulders beneath the surface, there are ways of harmlessly discharging the aggression. Instead of venting your wrath on family and friends, find an isolated spot, such as the middle of a field, on a hilltop, or perhaps beside a fast-flowing river or stream. Then take a deep breath and scream or shout with all your might, releasing the pent up jealousy, anger, hatred – or whatever it might be. If isolation is impossible (as is often likely), scream or shout into a deep pillow or cushion to muffle the sound, then beat the hell out of it with your fists or a cricket bat!

Unfortunately, people who most need to let loose in this manner are often too reserved to do so – rationalizing their fear by calling the exercise childish, undignified, or simply useless. A few may consider the exercise harmful, perhaps leading to a loss of self-control, or of one's sanity. Should this be so, then **Cherry Plum** may be indicated. Seek counselling or psychotherapy if you feel the need.

The Holly child: Holly is a most helpful Remedy during childhood, particularly when the first child is jealous of the new baby, for example.

HONEYSUCKLE
Lonicera caprifolium

A beautifully fragrant woody climber, found in woodlands, on the edge of forests, and in bushy places. The flowers of the variety used for the Remedy are reddish on the outside (not yellow as is most common), the inner surface white, but turning yellow on pollination. Blooms June–August.

Method of potentization: Boiling.

Key negative state: Nostalgia, homesickness.

Comparisons: Compare with **Clematis** whose thoughts are far away in the future, in happier times to come. **Walnut**, unlike **Honeysuckle**, feels the need to break with the past, but is finding the transition difficult.

Honeysuckle sits at the window dreaming of times gone by — of joy and laughter, tears and hardship, of missed opportunities, and regrets. While her body struggles to survive in the present, her mind wanders down the lanes of nostalgia. And as she drifts further and further into the past, her life energies begin to stagnate in the inky pool of reminiscence, and thus she experiences a great loss of vitality. There is the danger that she may lose all interest in the issues and demands of the present. By the same token, she pays no heed to the life which lies ahead.

The **Honeysuckle** Remedy is of great comfort to the bereaved, or to the elderly person living alone. Others needing **Honeysuckle** are those who may have moved home or changed their job and now regret the action, dwelling on how much they miss their old life. Interestingly, the Remedy can also help those who cannot bear the thought of growing old, and of losing their looks.

(In fact, the negative state of regret actually accelerates the ageing of the skin.)

Positive potential following treatment: The ability to retain the lessons taught by past experiences, but not to cling to one's memories at the expense of the present.

Other self-help measures: Make every effort to occupy yourself with the present: for example, take an interest in current affairs programmes on radio and television. In addition, take up activities which are 'grounding' such as gardening, dancing, cooking, pottery, keep-fit, or some other form of physical exercise.

Try always to plan ahead, looking forward to events such as a holiday, an outing – or a visit to a science museum!

Mix with children – *listen* as well as talk to them.

The Honeysuckle child: She may suffer homesickness whilst staying with relatives; or she may have disturbing dreams caused by a recurrent upsetting memory.

HORNBEAM
Carpinus betulus

A tree similar to the Beech, though smaller, reaching up to 19m. Found in woods and coppices. The pendant male and upright female flowers are green-brown, opening in April or May.

Method of potentization: Boiling.

Key negative state: Tiredness, weariness; that 'Monday morning' feeling.

Comparison: Compare with **Olive** whose exhaustion is more complete, born of physical and emotional strain as a result of a long illness or convalescence. With **Hornbeam**, it is always the *thought* of what lies ahead that causes the tiredness.

'Oh no, it's Monday,' groans **Hornbeam**, 'I don't think I can face another week at the shop. I feel even more tired this morning than I did before I went to bed last night.' Yet as soon as he begins work and becomes involved with his normal activities, the weariness disappears – until the next time!

In convalescence, **Hornbeam** is just the same, doubting that he has sufficient mental energy to return to work or simply to face the usual daily routine.

Positive potential following treatment: The ability and strength to cope with seemingly insurmountable difficulties. A renewed interest in life.

Other self-help measures: Make every effort to break your daily routine – take a different route to work; visit somewhere new at least once a week; read a different kind of book, magazine, or newspaper from usual; take up a sport or a new hobby, and so on.

The Hornbeam child: This Remedy will be helpful for the child who is mentally sapped after the excitement (or strain) of returning to school after the holidays, for example, or after an illness.

IMPATIENS
Impatiens glandulifera (I. roylei)

A tall imposing balsam, growing to 180cm in height. Found by rivers and streams. Flowers vary from palest to fairly dark pinkish-mauve, though only the pale mauve flowers are used for the Remedy. Blooms from July to September.

Method of potentization: Sun.

Key negative state: Impatience and irritability.

'For goodness sake let me do it', snaps **Impatiens**, 'you'll take

all day!' She is quick in mind and body, suddenly flaring up when events do not move as swiftly as she would like. She blows hot and cold, pushing others to the point where they begin to feel like galley slaves. Yet, unlike **Vine** or **Vervain**, she is the unwilling leader, preferring to work alone and at her own pace.

In her more relaxed moments she will listen to advice, for **Impatiens** is essentially wise and open to new ideas. However, great restlessness is her guiding impulse. She sees things in a flash, making major decisions before anyone else can draw breath. But she often takes on too much, thus depleting her own energies and becoming bad-tempered and irritable. Her life's lesson, of course, is to develop the virtue of patience.

Impatiens is included in the **Rescue Remedy** for its calming effect when trauma has caused a great deal of agitation.

Positive potential following treatment: Great empathy, patience, and tolerance, especially towards the shortcomings of others.

Other self-help measures: Practise relaxation and deep breathing exercises (see Chapter 7), and commune with nature as often as possible – a wonderful tranquilliser. Treat yourself to an aromatherapy massage once in a while.

For long-term benefits, take up yoga or Tai Chi, or try the Alexander Technique: the re-education of posture and movement in order that all potentials of mind and body can be used to their best advantage.

The Impatiens child: She is always irritable, constantly squabbling with other children, or prone to temper tantrums. (However, if there is self-injury, turn to **Cherry Plum**).

LARCH
Larix decidua

A tall graceful tree reaching up to 42m. Often found growing on the edge of hilly woodland. The male and female flowers appear on the same tree, golden yellow and bright red, respectively. The catkins (flowers) open in late March to early May.

Method of potentization: Boiling.

Key negative state: Lack of confidence.

Larch believes whole-heartedly that he is inferior to everyone else. Like a stuck gramophone record going round and round in the same groove, he utters the words 'I can't, I can't'. Self limitation has become deeply ingrained, reinforced by past failures. Always he stands in the shadows allowing others (who are often less talented) to take his place in the limelight.

Dr Bach described the **Larch** Remedy as the Flower that helps us become a little bolder so that we may plunge into life, seeking to our utmost; and in so doing, we may fulfil our purpose on Earth, which is to gain experience and knowledge.

Positive potential following treatment: Ceases to know the meaning of the word 'can't'. Becomes capable and determined; perseveres even when there are setbacks.

Other self-help measures: Seek counselling if necessary, and follow the instructions regarding Dreamwork (see Chapter 3).

Develop new skills by enrolling on an adult education course. Also, if you can afford to work without pay, do some voluntary work. The experience will be enriching, not only enhancing future job prospects, but more importantly, boosting your self-esteem.

The Larch child: Like the adult, he feels unable to venture on his own, has low self-esteem, and needs a great deal of gentle encouragement from his parents and teachers.

MIMULUS
Mimulus guttatus

An attractive creeping plant, abut 30cm in height, found growing in wet places, especially near shallow streams. The bright yellow flowers open in June to September.

Method of potentization: Sun.

Key negative state: Fear of *known* things such as flying, animals, public speaking, going to the dentist.

Comparison: Compare with **Rock Rose** whose fear is extremely acute – it may be the result of a terrifying accident, for example. The **Mimulus** fear is less acute and is of a general nature. However, if actually experiencing panic as a result of an encounter with the object of your fear, be it a spider, cat, or whatever, then take **Rock Rose** or **Rescue Remedy**. Regular doses of **Mimulus** will help to lessen, and eventually transmute, the fear.

Sensitive, retiring **Mimulus** sits in the corner, both hands clutching a glass of sherry to her chest. She would rather not be here but forceful **Vervain** has persuaded her to join the 'fun' of the office party. She finds the laughing, shrieking exuberance of the other members of staff intimidating. She looks longingly at the fire-escape door, planning her exit: down the iron steps, past the terrifying cat on the wall, to the safety of her cosy little room at the quiet end of town.

Positive potential following treatment: Quiet courage to face trials and difficulties; becoming understanding and supportive of others in a similar situation.

Other self-help measures: Follow the instructions regarding Dream-work in Chapter 3, and practise the aura strengthening visual-ization in Chapter 7.

If you suffer from a specific phobia such as fear of cats, fear of accidents, of ill health, open spaces, and so forth, you may also need to seek professional counselling. In addition, accept that sensitivity is a fine gift, and can be put to positive use such as counselling others or performing healing work of any nature.

Repeat the following affirmation before you go to sleep at night: 'I connect with my higher self which is love. Where there is love, there is no fear.'

The Mimulus child: She may fear the dark, other children, animals or even the swimming pool.

MUSTARD
Sinapis arvensis

A very common annual 30–60cm in height, growing in fields and by the wayside. The brilliant yellow flowers appear from May to July.

Method of potentization: Boiling.

Key negative state: Fluctuating cycles of black depression.

Mustard has everything anyone could ever wish for on the Earthly plane: a lovely wife, two beautiful children, no financial worries, and a wonderful home overlooking the sea; but for many years he has been victim to fluctuating cycles of melancholia. Without warning and for no apparent reason, a heavy black cloud descends upon him, stifling the sunshine and joy out of life. The mood may remain for days or weeks, until it eventually lifts as suddenly as it came, only to return again later in all its engulfing darkness.

Positive potential following treatment: Inner serenity; the ability to transmute melancholia into joy and peace.

Other self-help measures: It may at first seem like masochism, but by acknowledging and accepting the **Mustard** state for what it is – a chance for one's spirit to learn and grow – we may pass through the gloom towards the light of the higher self. By fighting the negativity, which is just like tensing up against physical pain, we only succeed in giving it more energy. So, instead, enter fully into the mood: read a sad novel, listen to melancholic music, indulge in nostalgia – the Flower Remedy will see you through.

Take up Tai Chi which also teaches the art of yielding to force in order to weaken it.

Counselling or psychotherapy will help if you feel you really cannot work through the depression alone.

The Mustard child: If a child is showing the symptoms described above do seek expert help as well as giving the Remedy. If your doctor can only prescribe drugs, consider consulting a holistic therapist or a reputable spiritual healer (contact one of the organizations in Urgent Addresses).

OAK
Quercus robur

The majestic English Oak can reach a height of 30m and is extremely long-lived, possibly up to eight hundred years. In the

past much of Britain was covered in Oak forests. The male and female flowers develop on the same tree, opening at the end of April to early May.

Method of potentization: Sun.

Key negative state: Despondency as a result of obstinate, relentless effort against all odds.

Hard-working **Oak** has reserves of energy and willpower which are truly amazing. She leaves other resourceful people such as **Vervain** and **Vine** in the shade. When despondency does eventually set in, as a result of unceasing effort, she refuses to give in to ill-health or adversity. Rarely does she seek advice or help, hiding her tiredness from others lest they should discover her 'weakness'. As a consequence, of course, her life is always an uphill struggle.

Unfortunately, such an attitude could lead to a nervous breakdown. Life's lesson for **Oak** is to realize that hard work and achievement has its place, but is not the sole purpose of our existence. We also need frivolity and those precious moments of gentle tears – like the soft summer rain that refreshes and revitalizes the parched meadows.

Positive potential following treatment: The ability to overcome all life's problems with courage; to become strong, patient, and full of common sense.

Other self-help measures: Seek some frivolity in life! In addition, take up yoga to encourage flexibility of mind and body.

The Oak child: Like the adult, she works very hard, viewing her schoolwork as some vital duty which must be done well at all costs. Unlike **Elm** who may momentarily lose confidence, **Oak** carries on, pushing herself to the limits of endurance even though it may have become useless. Consider deeply whether the child is being pushed by over-ambitious parents.

OLIVE
Olea europoea

A small evergreen tree native to the Mediterranean. Only wild trees are used for the Remedy. The small whitish clusters of flowers appear on the numerous thin branches in the spring, usually April or May, or according to the local climate.

Method of potentization: Sun.

Key negative state: Complete mental and physical exhaustion.

Comparison: Compare with **Hornbeam** whose weariness is more of the mind, that 'Monday morning feeling'. The **Olive** exhaustion is complete, of both mind and body, the result of over-exertion during childbirth, for example, or after a long illness.

'I get exhausted just thinking about what needs to be done,' says **Olive**. 'Even the short walk to the park seems like a marathon – at times I'm so tired I feel I might collapse.' Indeed, so great is his weariness even the things that once gave him joy are no longer pleasurable.

Positive potential following treatment: Peace of mind; vitality; a renewed interest in life.

Other self-help measures: Of course, if total exhaustion has become a way of life, and is not simply the result of a stint of hard work, do have a medical check-up and/or consult a well qualified holistic therapist such as a homoeopath or medical herbalist.

Look after yourself: get plenty of sleep, fresh air, sunshine, and adequate exercise – a revitalising combination. Eat sensibly, and practise the deep breathing, relaxation, and aura strengthening visualization (see Chapter 7).

The Olive child: The Remedy is invaluable to children during illness and convalescence, acting as a strengthener.

PINE
Pinus sylvestris

The only Pine indigenous to Britain, found growing wild in Scotland, but much planted elsewhere. Grows to a height of 36m, its bark is browny-red lower down, orangey-brown and flaky in the upper crown. Male and female flowers appear on the same tree; yellow and red respectively. Flowers May to June.

Method of potentization: Boiling.

Key negative state: Self-reproach; guilt.

Pine carries the burden of original sin in her heart – not only blaming herself for the mistakes of others, but also apologizing for her very existence, believing that self-punishment is her only chance of redemption.

'Ouch! I'm so sorry,' she says when someone treads on her toes, 'my fault for putting my foot in the way.' Or: 'Forgive me, but I've been short-changed – my fault for having distracted you.'

Unlike **Larch**, who will not try for fear of failure, **Pine** will often forge ahead, only to become depressed when she fails to live up to her own high ideals – which incidentally she would never impose upon others. Her life's lesson is to realize that regret is fine, but we must also forgive ourselves and learn from our mistakes. As Dr Bach wrote: 'No thoughts of past errors must ever depress us; they are over and finished and the knowledge thus gained will help us avoid repetition of them.'

Positive potential following treatment: The ability to feel regret rather than guilt; self-forgiveness; to take responsibility with a fair and balanced attitude.

Other self-help measures: In a meditative state, or whilst lying down deeply relaxed (see Chapter 7), ask that you may be given an animal (an imaginary creature) to love and nurture. It may be a rabbit, a kitten, a dog, an eagle, or even a dolphin. Whatever animal comes to mind, accept this as representing your higher self. Feed the creature, stroke its soft fur, smooth feathers or warm shiny back – radiate feelings of warmth and love. See that the creature responds joyfully to your touch. How could you ever punish such a beautiful being? Know that retribution is unnecessary, for your past mistakes are already forgiven.

Practise this visualization at least twice a week for as long as you feel the need. At other times, whenever guilty feelings rise to the fore, think of your creature.

The Pine child: This child tends to be the scapegoat in class, taking the blame for the mistakes of others, accepting the punishment without complaint.

RED CHESTNUT
Aesculus carnea

This tree is less robust than the Common or White Chestnut, reaching up to 18–25m. The strong rose-pink flowers appear in pyramidal clusters in late May or early June.

Method of potentization: Boiling.

Key negative state: Fear and excessive concern for the welfare of others.

It is perfectly natural to be apprehensive for our loved ones when they embark on some new or risky venture, or when they are ill, but the **Red Chestnut** type's fear is out of all proportion to the event: 'Oh my God! She's not back yet, she should have been home fifteen minutes ago. The train must have crashed!'

Indeed, **Red Chestnut** habitually worries about his loved ones, fussing and fretting, smothering them with his concern. Should little Johnny catch a cold, there is the fear that it may develop into pneumonia. If Susan does not phone at the stroke of six, he paces up and down like some tormented beast.

Red Chestnut is also the Remedy for those who feel distressed as a result of reading or hearing about some terrible disaster in another part of the world. Such individuals identify strongly with suffering (of animals as well as people) and experience a sense of overwhelming powerlessness. As Bach said, our negative thoughts harm not only ourselves, but also those to whom they are projected.

Positive potential following treatment: The ability to send out thoughts of safety, health, or courage to those who need them; to keep a cool head in emergencies; to remain calm both physically and mentally.

Other self-help measures: Practise the aura strengthening visualization (see Chapter 7). Train yourself to imagine the person for whom you feel concern safely enclosed within their own sphere of light. Try not always to imagine the worst – a plane crash, car accident, or whatever – instead, see the person in your mind's eye arriving home safely, and smiling!

The Red Chestnut child: He may have been given a great deal of responsibility at an early age, perhaps caring for a new baby; or he could be reflecting the attitude of a parent or guardian.

ROCK ROSE
Helianthemum nummularium

A low, spreading, shrubby plant found on chalk downs, lime-stone, and gravelly soils. The bright yellow flowers open, usually two at a time, from June to September.

Method of potentization: Sun.

Key negative state: Extremely acute state of fear, terror or panic.

Comparisons: Compare with **Aspen** whose fear is of the mind — that something dreadful is about to happen, but not knowing what it may be. The **Mimulus** fear is of *known* things — fear of loneliness or of animals, for example. The **Rock Rose** fear is sheer terror — so serious as to cause intense fear in those around.

The negative **Rock Rose** state of mind only occurs temporarily during a crisis: for example, when there is great terror at the site of a horrific accident. For this reason, **Rock Rose** is included in the **Rescue Remedy**. In fact, **Rescue Remedy** is more likely to be used in emergencies because many people carry a bottle of the Remedy around with them for such purposes.

Rock Rose is also helpful to those who suffer from panic attacks triggered by stress.

Positive potential following treatment: Great courage — a willingness to risk one's own life for others.

Other self-help measures: This is not usually possible in an emergency.

If you suffer from panic attacks, practise deep breathing, relaxation, meditation, and nature attunement (see Chapter 7); and Dreamwork (see Chapter 3). Counselling or psychotherapy may also be necessary.

The Rock Rose child: This Remedy helps the child who may wake screaming from a nightmare.

ROCK WATER

This is not a plant, but water from the spring at Sotwell, a short walk from Mount Vernon. Dr Bach found that the water contained healing properties for the eyes – though when prepared for the Remedy, it works on a different level. The spring water is potentized in June and July when the sun is at its greatest strength. Incidentally, any spring which is still left free and in its natural state (not the wells and springs over which chapels and shrines have been built) can be used for the Remedy.

Method of potentization: Sun.

Key negative state: A too rigid self discipline; repression and self-denial.

It is dinner time at the meditation retreat; the only proper meal of the day. **Rock Water** sits erect at the table, her short dark hair sculptured to perfection. While the others tuck into the vegetarian fare with ravenous delight, she looks on in silent disapproval. In stark contrast, pernickety **Rock Water** eats sparingly, avoiding the yoghurt and curd cheese lest the animal protein 'coarsen' her vibrations.

Though **Rock Water** would never openly criticize others, she tries to set a good example at all times, and is proud of her stringent lifestyle. Yet if the truth be known, her spirit yearns for the freedom of spontaneity, laughter and tears – for the sheer joy of living life to the full.

Of course, the **Rock Water** type is also recognized in the fanatical keep-fit enthusiast, or in the person who is always on a stringent diet. In fact, most of us need the Remedy from time to time, when our needs are consciously or unconsciously denied.

Positive potential following treatment: An open minded idealism; sufficient conviction not to be easily influenced by others. To radiate joy and peace, thus being a natural example to others.

Other self-help measures: Seek some frivolity in life! Allow yourself a few luxuries: a cream cake, a lie-in on a Sunday morning, a lazy holiday, a cheerful article of clothing, and so on.

Incidentally, if you are very disciplined in your dietary habits, you may be surprised to learn that it is actually beneficial to lapse occasionally! According to British nutritionist Celia Wright, for one day a week you can and *should* feast. Eat and drink anything you like – yes anything – chocolate, fried food, fizzy drinks, creamy coffee. This acts to surprise the liver into activity, for it has very little work to do when you are on a very pure diet.

The Rock Water child: Not a state normally associated with childhood, though the Remedy may help the pernickety eater.

SCLERANTHUS
Scleranthus annuus

A small, easily overlooked, wiry, rather bushy annual, 50–70cm high. Grows in cornfields on sandy and gravelly soils. The pale or darker green clusters of minute, petalless flowers appear between July and September.

Method of potentization: Sun.

Key negative state: Indecision, uncertainty, mood swings.

Erratic **Scleranthus** of the grasshopper mind never quite knows whether he is coming or going, always being swayed between two possibilities: 'Should I wear the blue shirt or the green?' he asks himself (for unlike **Cerato** he rarely seeks advice). Or: 'What on Earth am I going to tell her – yes or no?'

Even when he does make up his mind, he is certain to change it again. Thus, it is hardly surprising that others regard him as somewhat unreliable, or a time-waster.

In illness, true to form, **Scleranthus** cannot decide where in his body he feels discomfort, the symptoms tending to move about, first here then there, irritating his doctor beyond measure!

It is interesting to note that the Remedy can also be of help in motion or travel sickness.

Positive potential following treatment: The ability to make a decision quickly and to act promptly; to maintain poise and balance whatever the circumstances.

Other self-help measures: As for **Cerato**.

The Scleranthus child: Like the adult, he is subject to extremes of mood, crying one minute, smiling the next. During illness symptoms move about or swing from one polarity to the other: constipation then diarrhoea, hot then cold, ravenous hunger then loss of appetite, and so on.

STAR OF BETHLEHEM
Ornithogalum umbellatum

A slender-leaved plant related to the onion and garlic. It grows to a height of 15–30cm and is found in woods and meadows. The

flowers are striped green on the outside and brilliant white inside, opening only in bright sunlight. Flowers from April to June.

Method of potentization: Boiling.

Key negative state: Shock, both physical and mental.

Star of Bethlehem, the Remedy for shock, is regarded by many Bach Flower practitioners as the most important component of the **Rescue Remedy**, harmonizing with the other four Flowers, yet also triggering the action of the whole.

Although not a Type Remedy, **Star of Bethlehem** can help those who suffer from long term physical or emotional distress as a result of some past trauma. It may have been bereavement, divorce, disturbing news, or a distressing sight. In fact, practically everyone experiences in the course of life some shocking episode that he or she has been unable to cope with.

Phillip Chancellor cites some dramatic examples of the effect of emotional shock on the physical body. A previously healthy woman, for example, sat on the cellar steps during a bombing raid on London. After the raid, when she tried to stand up, she found she could hardly do so; her hips had become locked – literally frozen with fear. Her doctor subsequently diagnosed arthritis. Another woman developed a blinding headache when she was told that her daughter had been killed in an air-raid. She suffered from the headaches for many years until she was finally healed by the Bach Remedies.[8]

The effect of shock can also be so delayed that many years might pass before the full impact is felt. It may manifest as feelings of guilt, depression, anxiety, anger – or perhaps in the guise of some physical complaint.

Although it is best to treat shock as soon as possible, **Star of Bethlehem** can often be the catalyst required if shock has been sustained and can be identified as the cause of the trouble.

Positive potential following treatment: A neutralisation of the effect of shock, whether immediate or delayed.

Other self-help measures: Though not usually possible in an emergency, the following may be helpful for delayed reactions: aromatherapy massage (essential oil of neroli is often indicated); and spiritual healing (see Useful Addresses).

The Star of Bethlehem child: This Remedy can be given to newborn babies (perhaps in the baby's bath water) to help neutralize the shock of entering the world.

SWEET CHESTNUT
Castanea sativa

The tree can reach up to 30m in open woodlands and parks. As it matures, the thick, grey-brown, deeply furrowed bark begins to twist into beautiful spirals around the trunk. The sickly scented, pale yellow catkin-like flowers appear after the leaves, from June to August.

Method of potentization: Boiling.

Key negative state: Extreme mental anguish; the utmost limits of endurance; unable even to pray.

Comparisons: Compare with **Mustard** whose depression comes and goes like a black cloud, the cause unknown. The **Sweet Chestnut** depression is triggered by some life-shattering event, yet unlike the **Cherry Plum** state, does not lead to suicidal feelings. Like **Agrimony**, **Sweet Chestnut** tries to hide her distress from others.

Sweet Chestnut sits slumped against the wall, desperately and utterly alone, her life shattered into a million pieces. There is no more yesterday or tomorrow, merely a dark foreboding present. Even death itself offers no true release, for the pain touches her very soul . . .

That is the extent of the negative **Sweet Chestnut** state of mind. The Remedy helps to unfreeze time, allowing the sun to rise again. And as it becomes brighter, an image of hope and new life appears on the horizon: the Phoenix emerging from the ashes.

Positive potential following treatment: Hope returns; the end of torment is at last within reach. She has personal experiences of the true meaning of life, and/or of the Godhead.

Other self-help measures: Not usually possible in the acute stage, especially if one is trapped in a war zone, for instance, or caught up in some other catastrophe. However, during the recovery period, try to commune with nature as often as possible, and consider having some spiritual healing (see Useful Addresses).

The Sweet Chestnut child: The Remedy may be indicated for the child suffering mental anguish as a result of parental divorce or bereavement.

VERVAIN
Verbena officinalis

A rough hairy perennial, 30–60cm high. Widespread on dry,

grassy ground, especially on chalk and limestone. The spikes of small lilac-coloured flowers open from June to September.

Method of potentization: Sun.

Key negative state: Strain and tension as a result of over-enthusiasm; hyperanxiety.

Comparison: Compare with **Vine** who is pushy and domineering in order to achieve her own egotistical ends. **Vervain** is motivated by concern for the welfare of others; a desire to enthuse and convert.

Vervain is prone to over-enthusiasm, some might say fanaticism. He lives on his nerves and is quite unable to relax. As a consequence, he suffers from stiffness and muscle pain, and sometimes headaches or pain in the eyes. His guiding impulse is the urge to convert others to his way of thinking with nothing less than missionary zeal. Although it could be said that his heart is in the right place, in his eagerness to fight the good fight, he is apt to put others off by bombarding them with his arguments. Rarely does he listen to any other point of view. Incensed by injustice, he takes the side of the underdog, initiating pressure groups, standing on committees and, of course, writing to the prime minister daily!

His life's lesson is to realize that too much pressure only produces counterpressure and squanders one's own energies in the process. As Bach said, it is often by *being* rather than *doing* that great things are accomplished.

Positive potential following treatment: The ability to step back from time to time and to relax when necessary. The realization that others have a right to their opinions. The wisdom to change one's mind as a result of discussion and good argument.

Other self-help measures: Although deep breathing and relaxation exercises are needed, it may be easier to begin by taking up some form of physical activity which counteracts rigidity of body and mind, such as Tai Chi, yoga or a martial art. Also, try to commune with nature as often as possible.

Have some massage therapy or aromatherapy; or learn the Alexander Technique.

The Vervain child: This child is tense and frustrated, perhaps also hyperactive; has difficulty sleeping, or needs less sleep than average.

VINE
Vitis vinifera

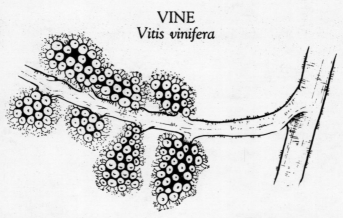

A long-lived climber, growing to a length of 15m or more. Indigenous to warmer countries such as Greece and the south of France. The flowers are small, green, and fragrant, appearing in the spring (according to the local climate, but usually May). Only the wild Vine is used for the Remedy.

Method of potentization: Sun.

Key negative state: A domineering and inflexible personality, always striving for power; ruthlessly ambitious.

Comparison: Compare with **Vervain** who tries to convince others through explanation and debate. **Vine** will not argue the matter, stating her point of view and expecting others to obey her command.

Vine rules her household like a warrior queen; the children – and even the dog – literally standing to attention whenever she barks her orders.

'Get that room tidied up this instant, otherwise you're grounded for a fortnight!' And then, to her husband, 'And you (**Pine**) should be ashamed of yourself! What kind of a man are you to let that moron get away with denting the car. Go and tell him, you wimp!'

At work, she is no different, terrorizing all those who dare to cross her path.

'Right, here's a parking ticket. You should have been back here one minute and thirty seconds ago precisely. It's more than my job's worth to let you get away with this.'

Interestingly, as Bach Flower practitioner Mechthild Scheffer points out, sometimes the negative **Vine** state appears together with weaker characteristics such as those of **Mimulus, Pine** or **Larch**. The weaknesses within the personality being over-compensated for by excessive will-power and hardness.

Positive potential following treatment: To become the wise and compassionate ruler, leader, or teacher who inspires others; to use one's great qualities of leadership to guide rather than to dominate.

Other self-help measures: For **Vine** even to recognize that she needs help is a great step forward indeed. She may only have reached such a state of awareness after being given the Remedy surreptitiously (in her tea perhaps) by her long-suffering husband!

Take up yoga or Tai Chi; follow the suggestions regarding Dreamwork in Chapter 3; and, if necessary, consider counselling or psychotherapy, particularly group work which encourages a sense of unity.

The Vine child: This child is always the leader of the gang, or the school captain; she tends to be aggressive, and in the extreme can become a bully.

WALNUT
Juglans regia

A beautiful tree reaching up to about 30m. Grows well in orchards and other protected places. The male catkins and small green female flowers appear on the same tree. Blooms in April and May, before or just after the leaf-buds burst.

Method of potentization: Boiling.

Key negative state: Difficulties adjusting to change of any nature. Oversensitivity to ideas and influences.

Comparison: Unlike **Honeysuckle**, **Walnut** desires to move on, but finds it difficult to break the link with the past, or with certain individuals.

The negative **Walnut** state is usually of a passing nature. It is the Remedy for those who have difficulty adjusting to a new situation, be it a change of job, a new home, a different country, a new faith, marriage, divorce, parenthood, or whatever. The Remedy helps to break the link with the past so that life can start afresh, free from old ties and memories. In fact, **Walnut** also proves useful in any physical change such as teething, puberty, pregnancy, and the menopause. Many women have found the Remedy helpful during the pre-menstrual phase. It is usually combined with **Scleranthus** (for mood swings) and with other Flowers accordingly.

    Walnut is also used by Bach Flower practitioners and healers alike as a means of 'psychic protection' (see page 108).

    Incidentally, though rare, it is possible to be a positive **Walnut** type. Indeed, Dr Bach himself has been described as a positive **Walnut** type. These people are the pioneers, inventors, and explorers of the world. They are usually very sensitive and idealistic.

Positive potential following treatment: Having the determination to carry through one's ideals and ambitions, despite adverse circumstances, damning comments and ridicule.

Other self-help measures: Read *Cutting the Ties That Bind* by Phyllis Krystal; and repeat the following affirmation before you go to sleep at night: 'I follow the guidance of my higher self.'

The Walnut child: As well as helping during the various milestones of a child's development (teething, starting school, and puberty, for instance), **Walnut** can help with adjustment to other changes; for example, staying away from home for the first time (with the grandparents perhaps), or when the child is suffering as the result of parental divorce or a major move.

WATER VIOLET
Hottonia palustris

A graceful, floating, almost hairless plant found growing in ditches and ponds, the finely divided leaves remaining under the surface of the water. The spikes of pale lilac-white flowers appear in May and June.

Method of potentization: Sun.

Key negative state: Pride and aloofness.

Water Violet stands alone, serene and self-contained. She is the wise teacher, the therapist, the peacemaker, the one who is sought after for advice. Yet her role is that of the listening counsellor rather than the assertive adviser, for she never attempts to interfere or influence, and similarly will not share her own problems or health concerns with others. Therefore, when unwell she prefers to be left alone. Likewise, she has been known to bear even the deepest grief with silent dignity.

A most admirable character indeed, many would say. True, but **Water Violet** runs the risk of becoming too self-contained and aloof; that same veil of superior separateness hardening into an impenetrable armour, thus isolating her from the rest of humanity. Others then tend to regard her as cold, conceited, or supercilious. As a consequence, she experiences the true meaning of loneliness within her self-built ivory tower of pride.

Positive potential following treatment: Although remaining comfortable with one's own company, one will have the wisdom and sympathy to put one's capabilities to the service of others.

Other self-help measures: Take up activites or hobbies which are 'grounding' – for example, gardening, sport, pottery, cooking, dancing, walking, giving and/or receiving massage.

The Water Violet child: Like the adult, rather proud and independent, an unusual child. She can spend many hours alone, playing contentedly.

WHITE CHESTNUT
Aesculus hippocastanum

The common Horse Chestnut tree can reach up to about 30m. The flowers are white with a patch of yellow-turning-to-red on the petal bases. The 'candelabra' clusters appear at the end of May to early June.

Method of potentization: Sun.

Key negative state: Persistent worrying thoughts and mental arguments.

Comparison: Unlike **Clematis** the daydreamer who is happy to escape from the world, **White Chestnut** would give anything to escape from his thoughts into the world.

White Chestnut suffers from a carousel mind, the same old arguments spinning round and round in his head, never reaching a satisfactory conclusion, interrupting his sleep, and causing a great deal of distress. He feels exhausted and is unable to concentrate. As a consequence, he can be somewhat accident-prone and tends not to hear when he is spoken to.

Positive potential following treatment: Peace of mind and a solution to one's problems.

Other self-help measures: Occasionally, an overactive mind leading to insomnia can be indicative of a deficiency of zinc coupled with an excess of copper and/or other nutritional deficiencies (read *The Wright Diet* by Celia Wright).

Commune with nature as often as possible, and combine this with a physical activity (if you are able) such as brisk walking, hill or mountain walking, swimming, cycling, and so on. Also consider taking up yoga.

The White Chestnut child: The Remedy has proved helpful to older children suffering from insomnia as a result of excessive study during the examination term.

WILD OAT
Bromus ramosus

A grass commonly found as a weed on arable land, in damp woods and thickets, and by roadsides. The flowers appear in July and August.

Method of potentization: Sun.

Key negative state: Dissatisfaction because one's true vocation has not been found. Boredom and frustration.

Comparison: Compare with **Scleranthus** who vacillates between two possibilities, even the most trivial. **Wild Oat** is uncertain about her life's mission, but is otherwise decisive and clear-headed.

Wild Oat is the rambling rover, something of a lost soul who has yet to find her true niche in life. She has travelled far and wide, lived one lifestyle then another, and has had a variety of jobs, yet still she searches for that elusive state known as fulfilment.

Her life's lesson is to realize the virtue of channelling her talents towards a single goal, for to scatter her energies in all directions serves only to sow the seeds of discontent.

Positive potential following treatment: The realization of one's true vocation.

Other self-help measures: Practise meditation to help focus your attention in one direction (see Chapter 7).

Repeat the following affirmation before you go to sleep at night: 'I follow the guidance of my higher self.'

The Wild Oat child: This child is usually very able but, like the adult, tends to scatter her energies, rarely identifying with any particular peer group.

WILD ROSE
Rosa canina

The 'English Rose' is widespread in sunny hedgerows and thickets, though rare in Scotland. The fragrant flowers are white, pale pink, or deep pink, opening singly or in groups of three between June and August.

Method of potentization: Boiling.

Key negative state: Resignation and apathy.

For many years **Wild Rose** has been awakened at 6.30am by

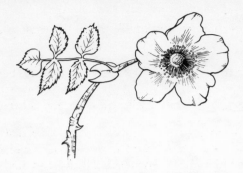

the jarring bell of the alarm clock. He gets out of bed like a zombie, feeling neither happy nor sad, neither lively nor depressed. After a cup of insipid tea and a slice of brittle toast, he trudges out of the house to the factory at the end of the street. Then he goes through the same old routine day after day – packing boxes of party hats and streamers, Christmas crackers and plastic novelty toys. At 4pm it's home again for tea, television and bed . . . and the start of another day.

That is the extent of the negative **Wild Rose** state of mind. He exists without joy or pleasure, making little effort to get well, or to find more congenial work. Uncomplainingly, he accepts illness, misfortune, and monotony as if they were a penance decreed by fate – for the 'sins of the fathers' no doubt.

Positive potential following treatment: A renewed interest in life and, with the return of one's vitality, the enrichment and enjoyment of friendship and good health.

Other self-help measures: As well as taking the Flower Remedies (a great step forward indeed), you may also need some other therapy to release the flow of vital energies – especially if the **Wild Rose** state of mind has been a way of life for some considerable time. Suggested therapies are: acupuncture, spiritual healing, colour healing, and psychotherapy.

The Wild Rose child: Do seek expert advice from your health practitioner if this state of mind has become chronic. It is common for a mild **Wild Rose** state to emerge during adolescence, though it is usually a passing phase.

WILLOW
Salix viminalis

A small tree reaching up to 10m found growing on moist and low-lying ground. The flexible branches are used for basket-making. In winter, the twigs turn a bright orange-yellow. The male and female catkins grow on different trees, opening in April and May.

Method of potentization: Boiling.

Key negative state: Bitterness and resentment; depression.

Comparison: Compare with **Holly** who is not a depressive by nature and can more easily express anger and jealousy. **Willow** is much more withdrawn and depressed, seeing herself as a victim – the 'poor me' attitude.

Sulky, grumbling **Willow** blames the rest of humanity or God for her 'miserable and cruel' lot in life. 'It's so unfair,' she mutters, 'I don't deserve this.' Yet never for a moment does she consider that her own attitude might be at fault. She has no interest whatsoever in others except to speak with bitterness and unkindness of their good fortune. Therefore, she considers it her 'right' to accept all kinds of help without a word of gratitude. Not surprisingly, she has succeeded in driving away many a friend or relative who initially offered her their help, understanding, and friendship. Of course, she will hold a grudge against such deserters for all eternity. Thus her distress turns inwards whereupon it eats away at her heart.

Many of us need a dose of **Willow** from time to time, especially on those days when nothing seems to go right and we begin to begrudge the happiness or good fortune of others.

Positive potential following treatment: Optimism and a sense of humour; the ability to accept responsibility for one's own life and health, and to see things in their true perspective.

Other self-help measures: Begin to take more responsibility for your own life and health by finding out as much as you can about the philosophy and practice of holism.

If you can afford to work without payment, take up some voluntary work, or offer to help your friends, relatives, or neighbours; for it is only by giving that we truly receive. Also, practise saying 'thank you', and progress to 'I love you'.

Commune with nature as often as possible; and see also the self-help exercise suggested for **Holly**.

The Willow child: She is sulky and resentful, but the reason for her distress is not always apparent. When lightly scolded for some misdemeanour, she feels she does not deserve so great a punishment.

RESCUE REMEDY

This is composite of five of the thirty-eight Flowers. As its name suggests, it is the Remedy for all emergencies – when there is panic, shock, hysteria, mental numbness, even unconsciousness. Although the Remedy cannot replace medical attention, it can alleviate much of the person's distress whilst they await the arrival of medical aid, thus enabling the bodymind's healing processes to commence without delay.

Rescue Remedy is also most helpful in other traumatic situations such as visiting the dentist, receiving bad news, attending court proceedings, after an argument, or when a child is distressed after seeing horror or violence on television, and so on.

Bach advised that we should carry a small bottle of **Rescue Remedy** with us at all times. It is also a good idea to keep a bottle in the bathroom cabinet or in the first-aid box.

The five Flowers which comprise the **Rescue Remedy** are:

Star of Bethlehem: for shock and numbness;
Rock Rose: for terror and panic;
Impatiens: for great agitation, irritability, and tension;
Cherry Plum: for violent outbursts and hysteria;
Clematis: for the bemused, faraway sensation that often precedes a faint, and for unconsciousness.

Dr Bach first used **Rescue Remedy**, in its original form which consisted of **Rock Rose**, **Clematis** and **Impatiens**, in 1930 – before he had discovered the other two Remedies. He gave it to a young man who had only just survived a shipwreck. The man was unconscious and blue in the face. As he was carried up the beach towards a nearby hotel, Bach moistened his lips, behind his ears and wrists with the Remedy. He gained consciousness before reaching shelter, and when he was put down there, he sat up and asked for a cigarette!

5

Dosages and Other Applications

THE UNADORNED ELEGANCE of the little dark-glass dropper bottles of Stock Concentrate reflect perfectly the gentle beauty and simplicity of Dr Bach's approach to healing. You can obtain the Stock bottles from most health shops, some chemists, or by mail order (see Useful Addresses page 119).

The Flower Remedies are modestly priced and economical to use: a little goes a very long way. For example, a 7.5ml size bottle of Stock, if diluted correctly, will provide approximately forty-five treatments. Moreover, the Stock Concentrates will keep indefinitely. However, once diluted in water for treatment, and stored in a cool place, they will keep for no longer than three to four weeks. Water does eventually turn stale, more especially tap water. For this reason, bottled spring or mineral water, which has a longer shelf-life, is recommended as a vehicle for the Remedies, although if this is unavailable, tap water will suffice. It might be a good idea to boil tap water first however, allowing it to cool before adding the Remedies. A teaspoon of brandy or cider vinegar added to the treatment bottle (see below) will act as a preservative, extending the life of the prepared Remedy for several more days.

PREPARATION OF THE TREATMENT

The standard dilution is 2 drops from each Stock Concentrate to a 30ml dropper medicine bottle (obtainable from most chemists) three-quarters filled with spring water and topped up with some brandy or cider vinegar. If a 30ml size dropper bottle is difficult to obtain, a slightly smaller or larger bottle will suffice.

Important: With **Rescue Remedy** (a composite of five Flowers) the dosage is doubled to 4 drops. Furthermore, when combined with other Flowers it is considered to be one Remedy. (See also page 91.)

DOSAGE

General Use

Take 4 drops of the diluted Remedy on the tongue 3–4 times daily. Alternatively, you can add the same number of drops to a small cup or glass of spring water fruit juice, or any other beverage. Incidentally, for acute conditions (see below), there is no need to prepare a treatment bottle, just add 2 drops of the Stock (4 of **Rescue Remedy**) directly into a glass or cup of spring water and sip at intervals.

It is most helpful to hold the dose in your mouth for a few seconds before swallowing, and to visualize the Flower vibrations flooding your whole being.

Babies and Nursing Mothers

The number of drops used for infant dosage (and for older children) is the same as for adults. 4 drops of the diluted Remedy is added to the baby's bottle, or taken in a teaspoonful of boiled water or fruit juice, 4 times daily. Nursing mothers can take the Remedies themselves, diluted in spring water. The Flower vibrations will then be imparted to the baby through the mother's milk.

Animals

Although not a panacea, **Rescue Remedy** is the main basic Remedy for animal treatment. Many animals given up for dead have revived simply by being given the **Rescue Remedy**. The normal dosage for domestic pets is 4 drops of **Rescue** (2 drops of any other Flower) in drinking water or milk, and some of this can also be sprinkled over the animals' food. For larger animals such as horses, 10 drops of **Rescue** (5 of any other Flower) to a bucket of water; or, if easier to administer, 4 drops of undiluted **Rescue**, 2 of any other chosen Flower, or on a sugar lump.

Plants

The Bach Centre suggests 10 drops of each chosen Flower to a large watering can. A plant that has been accidentally uprooted needs **Rescue Remedy** for shock, and probably **Walnut** too if it has to be transplanted. As a general garden tonic, especially when plants have become weakened by pests, a combination of **Rescue Remedy** and **Crab Apple** is recommended. In order to avoid over-watering, the drops can be administered daily in a dessertspoonful of water at the usual rate of 4 drops of **Rescue** and 2 of any other Flower. A tried and tested pick-me-up for cut flowers is a combination of **Walnut**, **Wild Rose** and **Rescue Remedy**. Add 4 drops of **Rescue** and 2 drops of the other Remedies to an average size vase.

EXTERNAL APPLICATIONS

Compresses

Bach prescribed compresses in addition to internal doses of the Remedies when there were external lesions such as skin eruptions and inflammation. 6 drops of Stock are added to half a litre of cold water. Place a small towel, or piece of lint or soft fabric, on top of the bowl of water. Wring out the excess and place the fabric over the area to be treated. Leave in place until it warms to body heat and renew as required.

Baths

Many Bach Flower users put the Remedies in the bath to augment oral doses of the same Flowers. For example: **Olive** or **Hornbeam** for exhaustion, **Crab Apple** for self-disgust or for skin problems.

Flower Remedy baths are also beneficial to babies and children – and even the dog! Add 5 drops of each chosen Stock Concentrate to the bath water.

Face Wash or Lotion

Crab Apple is commonly applied externally (combined with other treatment) for skin complaints such as eczema or teenage spots. Fill a 50ml bottle with distilled water or a 50/50 mixture of witch-hazel and distilled water, and add 2 drops of **Crab Apple**. Shake well before use and apply 2 or 3 times daily.

DURATION OF TREATMENT

There are no hard and fast rules about the length of time one should continue taking the Remedies. Treatment is always geared to individual needs. For acute conditions such as the effects of bad news (**Rescue** or **Star of Bethlehem**), that 'Monday morning' feeling (**Hornbeam**), or fearfulness before an interview (**Rescue** or **Mimulus**), for example, take the drops as often as needed. This could be every fifteen minutes or so until you feel better. Most people experience some relief almost immediately.

When dealing with deeply ingrained negativity – a domineering and inflexible personality, for example, or a tendency to possessiveness and self-pity – the process of change and a return to health may take many months. As each layer within the psyche begins to peel away like the many layers of an onion, different emotions will emerge, feelings we may have held in check for many years. Make a note of any negative change (of course, positive feelings will also come to the fore) and add the appropriate Remedy to the treatment bottle. There is no need to prepare a new bottle every time as a 30ml treatment bottle will last for about three weeks, but after a while it may be necessary to reassess the condition and to prescribe accordingly.

An indication of improvement is of course when we begin to feel better both physically and mentally and when our family and friends notice the difference – but more especially when we forget to take the Remedies! This means we are becoming less self-interested and beginning to flow outwards to others and the world about us.

USE OF THE RESCUE REMEDY

As we have seen, **Rescue Remedy** is usually for emergency situations, though it can be used as a long-term Remedy, in place of **Star of Bethlehem** for instance. For acute conditions such as shock or hysteria, put 4 drops from the Stock bottle into a cup or glass of water or any other drink. Encourage the person to sip the Remedy at intervals until the distressed feeling abates. If there is no suitable liquid available, the Remedy may be given neat, directly from the Stock bottle. Put 4 drops on the tongue as often as required. If the patient is unconscious, the drops can be applied externally, either diluted or directly from the Stock bottle. Moisten the lips, gums, temples, back of the neck, behind the ears, or the wrists.

As a first-aid measure – for example, for sprains, insect stings, bumps and bruises – apply the Remedy neat, or diluted in a little water. Alternatively, you can apply **Rescue Remedy Cream** which is available from the usual suppliers of the Remedies.

Important: Burns and scalds should always be cooled immediately under cold running water before applying the liquid **Rescue Remedy**. Do not use the cream in this instance. According to the first-aid authorities, it is not advisable to apply a fatty substance such as ointment to new burns, especially if they have not been cooled under running water, because ointment tends to fry on the skin, thus causing more pain and inviting infection. The **Rescue Remedy** given internally will, of course, deal with the shock. Obviously, serious burns need urgent medical attention.

6

Experiences in Bach Therapy

IT WOULD BE true to say that Bach intended the Flower Remedies to supercede homoeopathy proper, and perhaps also to replace some other forms of treatment. Homoeopathy embraces the principle of treating like with like, that is to say by administering minute quantities of a substance which, if given in larger doses, causes similar symptoms to the disease which it is employed to cure. According to Bach, the homoeopathic Law of Similars is born of an incomplete understanding of the nature of the whole, for disease itself is like curing like. The purpose of disease is to hinder and prevent us from carrying our negativity too far:

> It is a lesson to teach us to correct our ways and to harmonise our lives with the dictates of our soul . . . When the lesson of pain and suffering and distress is learnt, there is no further purpose in its presence, and it automatically disappears. [9]

Therefore, true healing occurs not by repelling disease with the darkness of substances of a similarly low vibration, but as a result of flooding our being with the light of a higher vibration in the presence of which, the disease – as well as the spiritual need for its existence – is eliminated.

Whatever the arguments for or against this view, the Flower Remedies in Bach's own hands undoubtedly proved most efficacious – indeed, miraculous on occasions. However, we need to consider how much of this can be attributed to Bach's own extraordinary gift of healing, and how much to the Flower Remedies themselves. In my own experience, which is mirrored by the many other therapists of different schools of healing who were interviewed, the Flower Remedies cannot totally negate the need for homoeopathy, or any other form of treatment for that matter, especially in serious or chronic illness. Nevertheless, the Remedies are extremely supportive, and on occasions can be sufficient in themselves, as the following brief case studies and anecdotes serve to illustrate.

SOME CASE STUDIES

Michael: Michael is in his mid-thirties. At the time of the consultation he was suffering from excruciating low back pain as a result of hard physical labour. He had refused to recognize his own limitations, and he also mentioned that he had strained his back in a similar manner on several other occasions. Although he believed his problem to be entirely physical in origin, it transpired that he had been feeling tense and anxious for some days before the accident. Yet again, he had received notice of redundancy from his work in conservation (the third such incident within two years).

Treatment commenced with aromatherapy massage. Michael was extremely tense; the muscles of his lower back were in spasm, and his neck and shoulders were also tight and painful. He expressed his dire need to get better quickly as he disliked taking sick leave, even though he had only two more months left with his job. I felt that he was not responding to my touch, and so at this point I interrupted the massage (not usually a good practice as it breaks the all-important flow) in order to give him a glass of water containing; **Impatiens** for his irritability, tension, and impatience to return to work; **Chestnut Bud**, because he had not learnt from past experiences of over-exertion; and **Star of Bethlehem** for the shock of losing his job.

Almost immediately I detected a change. He began to relax into the massage instead of fighting against it, his breathing deepened, and he became very sleepy. At the end of the treatment the pain had eased considerably. Within two weeks of taking the aforementioned Flower Remedies three or four times a day, and receiving aromatherapy treatments twice weekly, he began to feel more optimistic. Not only had the back pain diminished, but his haemorrhoids (from which he had suffered for years) had ceased to be troublesome! Careerwise, he has decided to go it alone: to run courses and workshops on the various aspects of conservation. Whenever doubt sets in he takes a dose of **Gentian** to keep him on the right track.

Judy: When I first met Judy she was struggling against all odds to hold down her job as a laboratory technician. At the age of thirty-two, she had been on Valium and anti-depressant drugs for nearly six years, from the time she had suffered a breakdown and subsequent hospitalization. Her story revealed an unhappy childhood, numerous love affairs in which she was usually the rejected partner, and a period of experimentation with various intoxicants. She expressed a need to be in control of her own life, for she felt like a piece of driftwood on a turbulent sea.

Judy's journey towards peace of mind was long and not without pain and set-back. However, within nine months she was beginning to see the light at the end of the tunnel. She had been receiving aromatherapy massage once or twice a month, as well as counselling, relaxation therapy, and the Bach Flower Remedies. With her doctor's permission and with the support of the self-help group Narcotics Anonymous she managed to give up Valium and to reduce considerably the dosage of the anti-depressant drug she was taking, though she experienced some harrowing withdrawal symptoms from the Valium.

A number of Remedies were given at various stages. These included **Star of Bethlehem** for past trauma and shock; **Larch** for lack of confidence; **Mimulus** for her fears; **Cherry Plum** and **Gentian** when she suffered a serious set-back and feared another breakdown. In addition, **Scleranthus** helped with the mood swings and unsteady gait experienced as a result of withdrawal from Valium; and **Agrimony** proved useful at times when she found herself putting on an overly cheerful front, which demanded an almost superhuman effort, in order to disguise from others her inner turmoil. However, the most interesting Remedy, the greatest catalyst for change, was revealed through Dreamwork.

Judy had been experiencing a number of dreams centred on the theme of advice-seeking. In one significant dream she found herself consulting an authoritative-looking man dressed in a pin-striped suit. He was seated on a throne. She asked him whether she should sell her car in order to buy a horse. She then found herself mimicking his gestures, facial expression, and even the sound of his voice, but when she awoke she could not remember the answer to her question.

The Remedy which sprang to mind was **Cerato**, the Remedy for the compulsive seeker of advice who ignores the wisdom of his own inner voice, and who also tends to mimic those whom he admires.

A few months later Judy had re-discovered her 'green fingers', and gave up her job to become a self-employed gardener. By that time she was also offered psychotherapy on the NHS (a rare opportunity) which she was pleased to accept.

Sylvester: Sylvester, an un-neutered tom-cat, turned up during the hard winter of 1990. By late spring of the following year, the vet diagnosed feline AIDS, though this was not confirmed by a blood test. At any rate, he was seriously ill and not expected to survive another week. However, I was not prepared to say goodbye to my new friend, and I felt that he too was not quite ready to take his leave. So home treatment went full-steam ahead. Healing was geared to nurturing both the physical and the spiritual aspects. The Flower Remedies played an important role, especially **Olive** and **Rescue Remedy**, along with homoeopathic doses of *Sulphur* and *Arsenicum album* at different stages of the illness.

Admittedly, this was a hit-or-miss affair as I am not a homoeopath. Essential oil of Tea-Tree (an anti-viral oil used in the holistic treatment of human AIDS sufferers[8]), was rubbed into his belly every other day. He was also given spiritual healing.

Within a week he began to show signs of recovery. Today, six months later, Sylvester is his lively mischievous self – though with his battle-scarred countenance, he will never be renowned for his beauty!

Jack: The following case study was contributed by Susan Morgan of Merthyr Tydfil, South Wales.

My husband Jack is fifty-three, a bus driver. For many years he has suffered from very itchy, weeping eczema on his hands and feet. The doctor prescribed various steroid ointments which seemed to help at first, but then made the rash even worse. Jack became so distressed by the itching and deep cracks in his skin that he decided to consult an alternative practitioner. He was tested for food allergies (by applied kinesiology) and also for the Bach Flower Remedies. The therapist put him on a milk-and-cheese-free diet and prescribed the following Remedies: **Rescue Remedy, Holly, Crab Apple** and **Chestnut Bud**. After six months he was amazed at the improvement, not only in his skin, but in himself. He certainly has a softer look in his eyes and a lighter step. It is as though a great burden has been lifted from his shoulders.

Lenny Sykes: Lenny is a practising homoeopath from Stratford-upon-Avon, England, who also employs the Bach Flower Remedies in her healing work. Although she sees the Flower Remedies as largely supportive, especially in chronic illness, she does recognize their role as sole healing agents for certain individuals and particularly in the healing of animals.

The Remedies proved remarkable in the case of her own dog who tended to be aggressive towards other animals, very fussy by nature, and terrified of water. Within three weeks of Bach Flower treatment, he no longer snapped at every dog in the neighbourhood, and even more surprisingly he went for a swim in the pond!

In addition to **Rescue Remedy**, other Flower Remedies chosen included **Mimulus** for his fear of water; **Holly** for his jealous behaviour to other dogs; **Crab Apple** for his fussy nature (he tended to lick his paws a great deal); and **Chestnut Bud** for his failure to learn from past encounters with ferocious dogs!

Lenny has also found the Remedies extremely beneficial in her own illness. For many months she had suffered from ME (Myalgic Encephalomyelitis), a debilitating illness associated with immune dysfunction, for which there is no orthodox cure. Symptoms include depression, short-term memory loss, general aches and pains, and an overwhelming fatigue. Although she was taking homoeopathic remedies, the Flower Remedies proved to be a wonderful adjunct, helping to uplift her spirits during the inevitable down periods. She found **Gorse** indispensable in this respect. Moreover, Lenny, in tune with many other homoeopaths, believes the Flower Remedies lessen the uncomfortable, though temporary, aggravations sometimes caused by the high potency homoeopathic remedies which are usually prescribed for chronic conditions.

Although at the time of the interview Lenny had not fully recovered, she was well on the way to perfect health. She expressed an enthusiasm to specialize in the healing of animals and is an ardent supporter of the well-known homoeopathic vet, George Macleod.

Violet: This case study is about personal growth rather than the treatment of illness, and due to lack of space, this is a condensed version of the original account contributed by Judith Kidd who practises near Abergavenny in South Wales. Judith uses the Flower Remedies in conjunction with Reflex Zone Therapy of the feet (reflexology) and Aura Soma colour healing, a method which employs coloured oils infused with herbal extracts and essential oils potentized by crystals.

Violet was a middle-aged woman, unusual in that she expressed most of her problems to Judith by relating her dreams. This she would not have done had she not been inspired by the Aura Soma coloured bottles on display in the window of the treatment room. The colours triggered within her the realization that Judith would not regard her as mad should she talk of her strangely powerful, often prophetic, dreams.

The first dream she related was most interesting. Violet's spiritual guide had taken her back in time to when the Earth was young. There she was shown exquisite flowers, and colours of an unfamiliar hue. She became aware of two major tribes of people: one dark and short, the other taller, fair, and better looking. She found she could understand their languages. She did not wish to leave this fascinating world, but her guide insisted that it was time to return. So she entered a rocking boat which sailed her home.

From the discussion that followed, it transpired that Violet was unhappy with her mundane life. As a wife and mother, she had always devoted her time to caring for her family, rarely considering her own needs. When Judith asked what might bring happiness into her life, Violet said she would like to paint.

She then went on to describe the circumstances of her first unhappy marriage and the distress that this had brought to her three children. She was also burdened by the guilt she carried for her daughter who was anorexic. (Judith believes that a domineering father is sometimes implicated in cases of anorexia.)

Before meeting her second husband, Violet had a very vivid dream. She found herself in the house of a sick woman who was lying on a double bed in a downstairs room. Moved by the woman's suffering, Violet sat on the bed and comforted her, holding the woman in her arms until she fell asleep. Then the sick woman's children passed by the bed, refusing to acknowledge their presence . . .

The meaning of this dream soon materialized: Violet's second husband had nursed his sick wife until her death. She had passed away on the double bed that he had moved downstairs. As the dream had so clearly illustrated, his children were extremely selfish, having no consideration either for their mother or for Violet.

Judith prescribed **Walnut** to enable Violet to experience change in her life and a growth of understanding. She also gave **Pine** for feelings of guilt and self-reproach and to enable her to accept the situation. In addition, she was given **Indian Paint Brush** (not a Bach Remedy, but a Californian Flower Essence) which would help her to express herself artistically.

Over a period of a few months, Violet began to feel more relaxed and positive, and she converted the spare room in her house into a studio. By working at what she enjoyed doing most she had discovered a new identity and was able to view her problems from a different, less painful perspective.

Bach Flower user Heather Weaver from Shropshire, England, kindly contributed the following anecdotes.

Leonard: We found Leonard, our neighbour's cat, dragging himself up our drive one afternoon. His lower back was paralyzed and his rear legs useless. We suspected he had been hit by a car. He was dazed, hardly knew where he was, and reminded us horribly of one of those ghastly nodding dogs one used to see in the rear windows of cars. We dropped **Rescue Remedy** on his nose and paws which he instinctively licked away. We also gave him a **Rescue Remedy**-medicated saucer of water to drink before his owner took him to the vet. There the vet remarked that the only thing inconsistent with his having had such a traumatic accident was that the animal was not in shock and he could not understand why . . . So much for the placebo effect!

Heather: I felt that I was being put upon somewhat in my workplace so I decided to take **Centaury** to help counter my 'doormat' tendency. Two nights later I experienced a welcomed side-effect: my unsuspecting partner appeared with some domestic queries and I found myself saying, '. . . and by the way Paul, I'm not going to cook dinner twice to your once any longer so you'd better find another dish by the end of the week.' Rather than suffer his egg extravaganza (his sole *pièce de resistance*) every other evening, I'd volunteered to cook two evenings to his one until he found another recipe. It amazed me when I realized this had been going on for six months. The **Centaury** helped me to assert myself in an area of my life where I'd not consciously observed that I was being exploited.

Let us conclude this chapter with an unusual account contributed by Sophie Richards, a musician from London.

Sophie: Apart from the undeniable specific results which could only be attributed to the Remedies (for sometimes I did not know which Remedies had been prescribed until I had reported to my therapist their 'text book' effects), I became aware of another aspect. Unexpectedly I experienced some vivid sensations which could only be attributed to 'aura'.

Years earlier I had tried to understand and to see auras, but felt I had never done so. Now, unintentionally, almost as a side-effect of the Remedies, I began to encounter a very real experience of my own aura. I can only describe it as a gentle, almost fluid, ethereal substance which radiated from my skin and seemed to lighten and refine my whole being.

I found the Remedies not only strengthened my own aura, but at times this seemed also to have a direct and specific effect on the well-being of others with whom I came into contact – specific in that the effect was in accordance with the particular Remedy taken. On one occasion a Remedy I had taken seemed to work on a colleague before it actually had an effect on me! (See also page 108.)

7

Towards Whole Health

ACCORDING TO THE principles of nature cure (naturopathy), and indeed of holistic therapy in general, the food we eat, the water we drink, the air we breathe, the seasons, and even the phases of the Moon can affect the way we feel. Therefore, by influencing our moods, these things must also affect our physical state.

In truth, as Bach said, 'Nothing can hurt us when we are happy and in harmony'. However, perfect equilibrium between mind, body and spirit is not easy to attain – at least not as a permanent state of being. Yogis and great spiritual teachers have achieved such an ideal, but most of us will be held in check by many factors such as lack of incentive, weakness, heredity, karma (fate or destiny), or whatever. And there is always the possibility of some life-shattering event around the next corner which is certain to tip the balance.

However, as most physicians and holistic therapists would agree, a well-nourished, cared-for body will usually fare much better and respond more readily to whatever treatment is given, than one which is congested with cigarette smoke, junk food, and the debris of an unhealthy lifestyle. This is not to undermine the ultimate superiority of the mind/spirit – some people fail to respond to treatment despite doing everything 'right'. Rather, it is to suggest that the physical aspect, being an interrelated part of the whole, needs to be nurtured by material as well as spiritual means. Of course, at the vibrational or quantum level (refer back to Chapter 2) there is no true separation of mind, body, and spirit, but we *perceive* a separation because the Whole (like trying to picture the infinity of the Cosmos) is beyond our personal experience.

As a matter of interest, not only is it possible for our physical state to influence our moods, but in extreme cases it can affect our sanity. Certain forms of schizophrenia, for instance, can be triggered by allergies to substances such as coffee, wheat gluten, and alcohol.[11]

Then there is the question of pre-menstrual tension, or PMS as it is now called. A few esoteric healers, though not Dr Bach, have suggested that the condition is a 'rejection of the feminine processes'. This rings of Freud's 'penis envy' – another fallacy? While it may be true in a few cases, surely it cannot be so for the many thousands, and possibly millions, of women who suffer from PMS? It is my own belief that a certain *degree* of PMS, and I do not include suicidal or murderous tendencies here, is a perfectly reasonable response by a healthy reproductive system to the unnatural state of non-pregnancy. Of course, I am not saying that women should give in to biology (perish the thought) but that PMS is at least partly physical in origin (unless one views contraception or celibacy as a rejection of the feminine processes). The real culprit, as far as we on the Earthly level of awareness are concerned, is fluid retention, caused by natural changes in body chemistry. PMS is also exacerbated by stress and a poor diet which is why it can, to a great extent, be remedied, – as so many women have discovered.

In a nutshell, all truly holistic therapies seek to strengthen the bodymind's own innate self-healing ability. Even though some people are born healthier than others, most of us can become healthier and prevent the development of the so-called diseases of civilization such as bowel cancer, diabetes, and heart disease. The key to good health and a sense of well-being lies in the realization that we need not be helpless victims of stress or *distress* which account for a great many ills. While our diet and lifestyle play a part, we need also to nurture our spiritual aspect, for we are more than a mind and a body.

The spiritual aspect is hard to define but is tied up with our relationship with ourselves, with other people, with our own sense of purpose and meaning, and indeed with the health of our Planet. Without purpose we become depressed or apathetic; life then appears bleak and meaningless. Even when we do not follow a conscious spiritual path in terms of a religious faith, we may in fact be realizing our purpose in some other way. It could be through music or some other art form, no matter how humble, or simply through our work, family, relationships, or through a love of animals or nature – or more actively perhaps by working towards the realization of a humanitarian or Green ideal.

The vision of the truly holistic healer (which must include Bach), and indeed of all those within the Green Movement, is that the expression of such qualities as compassion, intuition, and nurturing will raise the consciousness of humanity as a whole. In so doing, we will once again begin to honour the Earth, as did the healers of antiquity, realizing that we and the Earth move together in the one Dance of Life. However, putting intuition back into medicine does not mean we have to go completely overboard into the realms of Earth magic at the total expense of logic. There needs to be a marriage between the two seemingly opposing principles – between the archetypal 'feminine' and 'masculine'. In other words, we need to integrate science with mysticism, and the best of orthodox medicine with the best of the gentler approaches. For as day cannot exist without night, nor the Sun without the Moon, logic is dehumanized without the balance of intuition and feeling.

PUTTING IT INTO PRACTICE

The rest of this chapter is devoted to outlining some suggestions for creating favourable conditions within every level of our being, for in so doing we may enhance the action of the Flower Remedies. You are of course free to accept, disregard, modify, or improve upon any of these mindbody exercises or activities according to your own needs or level of awareness.

The Nature of Stress

Unlike sheep, we humans need a high level of stimulation in order to motivate us and keep us going. Indeed, without 'the spice of life' we begin to feel despondent, or apathetic – remember **Wild Rose?** Conversely, when the demands of life exceed our ability to cope effectively, we begin to suffer the effects of overload. In either situation, we experience *distress* which can pave the way towards illness.

Stress is not so much the outside pressures and problems which impinge upon us but rather how we react to those things or people 'out there'. We all know people who remain cool, calm, and collected under the most trying circumstances, and we know others who collapse under the strain of even relatively minor difficulties. The trick is to find and maintain just the right level of stress to make our life interesting and fulfilling, and of course this balance is different for each individual.

If your life is understimulating, make every effort to break the routine. This may sound obvious, but is easy to overlook when you are in a rut. Visit new places as often as possible; follow up sudden notions; take up a new hobby; provide for compensatory physical activity such as walking, cycling, swimming, and so forth.

In fact, in relation to both types of stress, regular though moderate exercise stimulates the circulation, which in turn increases oxygen levels in the blood. This has a definite positive effect on our state of mind. Anyone who has recently taken up some form of exercise, especially something they actively enjoy, will tell you that it has brought them enhanced mental energy and concentration, the ability to sleep more deeply, and a feeling of well-being. Swimming, walking and simple dance are arguably the most natural, and therefore the most beneficial, forms of movement.

However, if you are elderly, physically disabled, or too ill to take much exercise, regular massage (if carried out with sensitivity) can be of enormous benefit to body, mind, and spirit. Indeed, massage is a wonderful therapy for all of us, regardless of whether we are suffering from stress.

Nature Attunement

Nature in her myriad forms is perhaps the most potent de-stresser of all – a simple fact so often over-looked by many experts in the field of 'stress management'. She offers tranquillity to the frenzied, and raises the spirits of the down-hearted. All that she asks in return is a little of our time and attention. Although we may love city life, we can, without realizing it, become very much out of balance when cut off from the natural Earth currents.

If you can only occasionally leave the city in order to visit the countryside, sea, or mountains, do not despair: even the local park can be a source of healing. Try to take time out each day (at least half an hour) to breathe in the scents of flowers, trees, and grasses; to listen to the birds; to feel the rough bark of a gnarled oak; to walk on the soft earth, and to embrace the elements. Do not be afraid of the wind or the rain, snow or frost. Wrap up warmly so that you need not hunch up against the cold, thus creating further tension. Let go – and enjoy!

As you may know, when the American Indians became ill, one of the first things they did was to enter the forest where they would sit with their back against the trunk of a mature tree. In this way they 'grounded' themselves, 'sitting in the lap of Mother' as they put it, to receive healing. Likewise, we too can benefit from this simple practice.

Incidentally, if you are taking one of the tree Remedies (**Oak, Hornbeam, Red Chestnut**, or whatever) try to find the appropriate tree with which to attune. Breathe deeply and allow yourself to merge with the energies of the tree. Similarly, you can attune to the vibrations of any other Remedy plant such as **Gorse, Mimulus, Impatiens**, or **Honeysuckle**. Much of the joy of this exercise is in the seeking and finding of the Remedy plants. Even when not in bloom, silent contemplation of the plant or tree can be a healing experience.

Silent contemplation of moving water is another beautiful attunement. Close your eyes and listen to the music of a running stream, flowing river, waterfall, or the waves of the sea. If you live far from any natural source of running water, an ornamental fountain in a park or garden can be of equal value.

For the physically able, what better way to commune with nature than to spend some time in the wilderness? There is something special about climbing a mountain, especially for the first time, or camping on the edge of a forest by a running stream, or walking on the remote high cliffs in summertime – the wind in your hair, the scent of wild flowers, the springy turf underfoot, and the air resonating with the symphony of seabirds and crashing waves . . . There is something special indeed, something mystical yet profoundly real, about coming close to the Earth.

Seeking Within

As well as communing with nature, you may also enjoy practising a more conscious form of mindbody healing in the form of deep breathing, relaxation, visualization, and meditation. By learning to connect with your inner powers you will tap a source of self-healing which will resonate in harmony with the Bach Flower vibrations. After a while, you will begin to find that you are reacting less self-destructively to the pressures of life, becoming more resourceful in the face of adversity. It is a fact that the mindbody can either trap or liberate the spiritual aspect of self. The condition of spiritual imprisonment or freedom depends on many interrelated factors, but especially on how we breathe and think. Although we cannot always change our outer situation, we can change our attitude to it, which makes all the difference in the world:

> Two men look out through prison bars,
> The one sees mud, the other stars . . .
>
> Anon

Breathing The power of the breath has always been associated with an energy of both a physical and a metaphysical kind. According to the yogis, and no doubt also to adepts of other schools of mysticism, the breath is the key to spiritual transformation. Even in the Bible, the word translated as 'spirit' can also be translated as 'air'. It is the invisible life-force. To the Chinese, who attempt to manipulate it in acupuncture, it is *Chi*; to the Aborigine it is *kuranita*; to the Polynesian, *manas*; to the yogi, it is *prana*.

As breathing is the only bodily function that can be either voluntary or involuntary (at least up to a point), it can form a bridge between the conscious and the unconscious. By influencing our breathing, we can change our energy levels and our mood. To illustrate this, start to breathe shallowly; pant in and out very quickly for about half-a-minute. At the end of this time you will feel decidedly anxious – your heart will be pounding and you may even be experiencing fear. As an antidote, take three or four long, deep breaths from the abdomen and exhale slowly. You will find your mind and body sinking into a state of calm.

Many of us are shallow breathers; we use only the upper part of our lungs, which means that toxic residues are not completely removed. As a result, the blood is deprived of much of the oxygen it needs to feed the body tissues, so we may end up feeling listless or suffering vagueness of thought. At the same time, the oxygen deficit hinders the assimilation of nutrients from the food we eat.

One of the easiest ways to begin learning to breathe fully, is to practise the yoga 'complete breath'. This exercise is also very beneficial to those suffering from respiratory ailments such as asthma, hay fever, and bronchitis.

1. Lie on a rug on the floor (or on the ground if outside, perhaps in a garden), or alternatively on a firm bed, with your arms at your sides, several centimetres away from your body, palms facing down.
2. Close your eyes and begin to inhale very slowly through your nose. Expand your abdomen slightly, then pull the air up into the rib-cage, and then your chest. Your abdomen will be automatically drawn in as the ribs move out and the chest expands. Hold for a few seconds.
3. Now begin to breathe out slowly through your nose in a smooth continuous flow until the abdomen is drawn in and the rib-cage and chest are relaxed. Hold for a few seconds before repeating two or three times.
4. Now breathe in slowly as you did in Step 1 but gradually raise your arms overhead in time with the inhalation until the backs of your hands touch the floor.
5. Hold your breath for ten seconds while you have a good stretch, from fingertips to toes.
6. Slowly breathe out as you bring your arms back down to your sides. Repeat two or three times.

This exercise can also be performed whilst standing. To enhance the stretch (Step 5) stand on tiptoes, your heels coming back down again as you breathe out.

Deep Relaxation   Deep relaxation is a prerequisite to the art of visualization and meditation. By inducing a slight shift in consciousness, deep relaxation enhances our ability to concentrate and to use imagery for self-healing – and indeed for the healing of others. Most interestingly, it is the key which opens the door to the wisdom of the higher self.

Before you begin, find a quiet, well-ventilated room with a pleasantly relaxing decor. Wear loose, comfortable clothing, and take off your shoes. If you live in a noisy area, it may also be helpful to play a tape or record of gentle music, but keep the volume down very low as your senses will be especially acute. Most important, ensure that you will not be disturbed for at least fifteen minutes.

On the subject of decor, according to colour therapists, the jarring vibrations that emanate from zig-zig patterns, or from vivid, clashing colours such as salmon-pink with bright orange, or yellow with scarlet, can affect us even when our eyes are closed. Neutral colours or pastel shades are much more conducive to relaxation and meditation.

1. Lie down on the floor or on a firm bed supported by pillows if desired – one under your head and another under your knees which will support your lower back.
2. Close your eyes, take one or two deep breaths through the nose, then breathe out through the mouth with a sigh . . .
3. Now become aware of your feet. Inhale through the nose, tighten your feet by first pointing your toes, and then flexing the feet towards your body. Hold on to this tension for a slow count of five, then let your feet relax as you breathe out through the mouth with a deep sigh.
4. As you inhale, tense your calves as you count slowly to five. Now let them relax as you breathe out with a sigh.
5. Progress to your knees, then your thighs, buttocks, abdomen, chest, shoulders, hands, arms, neck, head, and face. Tense each part as you hold the breath, then let it go as you breathe out with a sigh through the mouth, experiencing a wonderful sensation of release.
6. Take three deep breaths, inhaling from the abdomen, but without straining. Hold each breath for a few seconds, then slowly exhale through the nose.
7. Now become aware of your body and 'feel' around your body with your mind for any areas that may still be tense, and repeat the tightening and releasing of the muscles until you feel deeply relaxed and at peace.
8. When you feel ready (after at least five minutes of lying quietly and breathing normally), have a good stretch from fingertips to toes before slowly getting up.

This exercise is most beneficial if practised once or twice a day on an empty stomach, or at least half-an-hour after eating a light meal or snack.

PSYCHIC PROTECTION

Even though we may choose to overlook the fact, to a greater or lesser degree we humans are sensitive to the energy fields of others in our sphere. How often for instance, have you felt inexplicably uneasy in the presence of another? Conversely, have you ever experienced a sense of joy, or been uplifted in the company of an unusually vibrant person?

Some sensitive souls pride themselves on the fact that they can only mix with other similarly 'developed' people because the 'lesser evolved' make them feel uneasy. These same types often complain of feeling drained after travelling by bus or on the Underground. In truth, a person with a properly harmonized aura can go anywhere and mix with anyone without feeling any the worse for the encounter. Indeed, fear and anxiety weaken the energy field, producing an unhealthy, uncontrolled form of auric sensitivity. Moreover, contrary to what some people may believe, a strong aura is not the same as 'armouring'. In other words, it is not an impenetrable barrier cutting us off from others and the outside world; rather it acts as a filter, allowing only that which cannot harm us to enter. By learning to strengthen our own vibrations, we help to uplift the spirits of those who may seek our help. We will still be sensitive to atmospheres and to the needs of others (perhaps more so), but we will not absorb negativity like a psychic sponge, thus draining our own energies in the process.

Strengthening the Aura

The aura is largely a thought emanation and as such can easily be controlled by thought. It is often helpful to begin learning to control and strengthen the aura immediately after practising the complete breath and/or the relaxation sequence outlined earlier.

Whilst standing, or lying on your back, close your eyes and take a few long, slow, deep breaths. Then imagine that you are centred within a sphere of white light which also permeates your body. Feel that you are protected within this sphere of light like the yolk within an egg and that the energy around you is unbroken, especially over your head. Some people think of blue or golden light; others may not think of a colour at all but just *feel* they are centred within a sphere.

With practice, this visualization, or feeling, of your auric space will become second nature. It can be carried out at any time you feel the need without first having to do the breathing or relaxation exercises. Think of your aura when you are near anyone with a cold or flu; when you or others are indulging in negative emotions; in noisy surroundings; first thing in the morning and last thing at night; after meditating or giving Bach Flower counselling.

Another way to dissipate uncomfortable feelings absorbed from others is to take a dose of **Rescue Remedy** and **Walnut** in a glass of water. In fact, water itself helps to cleanse the aura, so a bath or shower will also be helpful. Alternatively, dig the garden or go for a brisk walk in the park or countryside – the Earth will absorb or 'ground' any lingering discomfort.

Creating a Healing Channel

If it feels appropriate to you, the following visualization will be most helpful if practised a few minutes before each consultation.

1. Either standing or lying down on a firm but comfortable surface, take several complete breaths (see page 106).
2. Close your eyes and think of your aura as in the previous exercise. Then imagine that you are centred along a straight line running from the top of your head to your feet (this is known as 'centring'). Feel perfectly balanced and calm.
3. The next stage is to become a *channel* of healing energy – not the *source* as this would only serve to drain your own vitality. To become a channel, imagine (or feel) a source of energy above your head, a ball of white light or the Sun. At this point you can either address your higher self or say a prayer asking that you may draw down cosmic energy (or be given the ability) to help the person in the way best suited to their specific needs.
4. Now take a few deep breaths. As you inhale, imagine you are drawing energy from the source of light, in through the top of your head, and out through your hands and feet as you exhale.

During the consultation, you might also find it helpful to imagine that you are both centred within the same sphere of white light (some therapists prefer to imagine a triangle) above which is placed a symbol of protection. Symbols most commonly used include an equidistant cross within a circle, a white rose, or an ankh (a tau cross with a loop on the top, symbolizing eternal life). The visualization can be carried out in an instant, without its being obvious to the other person (not everyone will feel comfortable with this approach). However, if the person is amenable to intuitive healing, all well and good. They too can think of their own aura, and then merge their energies within the greater sphere or triangle of light.

At the end of the consultation, send a closing thought to the other person; see that they are separate from yourself, safely enclosed within their own spiritual sphere.

Now separate and ground yourself; that is, think of your own aura, see yourself centred along a straight line as before, then become aware of your feet in contact with the ground. If necessary, excuse yourself for a few moments in order to carry out this visualization.

The power of thought is everything. If you are able to do this successfully, and if there is an empathy between yourself and the other person, not only will your intuition and counselling skills be enhanced, but the experience will be healing for both parties.

Reflective Meditation

This is an *active* form of meditation as taught by the Pegasus Foundation (my own teachers) based in Malvern, England. Many Eastern approaches are *passive* in that they aim either to empty the mind or help us to become observers of our own thoughts – a most difficult task for the beginner. Reflective meditation, on the other hand, involves thinking about a definite subject, theme, thought, or word.

The following meditation can be recorded on to tape, but do allow plenty of pauses for the visualizations marked thus: . . . Or you might be able to persuade a friend with a soothing voice (most important) to guide you through it. Meditation should ideally be practised for fifteen to twenty minutes daily, preferably first thing in the morning. However, even as little as two or three sessions a week can help to reduce stress, improve concentration and encourage creativity and inspiration.

The Oak Tree   Before you begin, sit comfortably in a quiet room, or in a garden if you prefer. A cross-legged position may be adopted if you are accustomed to this position, otherwise sit in a straight-backed chair with your feet firmly on the ground and your hands resting in your lap.

1. Close your eyes. Empty your lungs and begin to breathe deeply through your nose. Do not strain, simply become aware of the breath as it flows in and out . . . (two minutes).
2. Concentrate on your feet; let them go, thinking relaxation into them . . . now move over every part of your body in turn, letting go and relaxing your calves . . . knees . . . thighs . . . hips . . . abdomen . . . now your chest . . . hands and arms . . . shoulders . . . neck . . . now your face . . . your eyes . . . your forehead . . . your scalp . . . even your tongue.
3. Now feel that you are centred within a sphere of white light – your aura . . .
4. Picture a majestic gnarled Oak standing in a lush green meadow; tall, strong, and in full leaf. See the width of its deeply furrowed trunk; the dark hollow in its base – the hiding place of many a small child. Look up into the dark green canopy. Consider how this ancient giant grew from a tiny acorn over many years; how its ancestors provided fruit for the wild boar, fuel and shelter for human beings. There is yet another gift from the Oak: a most precious gift which emanates from its pale yellow catkin flowers – a power to heal and comfort you when the responsibilities of life become a burden too great to bear alone. The Oak bestows upon you the virtue of strength in the face of adversity, helping you to overcome all life's uncertainties with courage and steadfastness . . .
5. Now feel the rough bark of the Oak . . . In that roughness there is a soft smile, a gentle smile like that of a loving, weather-beaten father who has worked hard to protect you, child of the Oak . . .
6. Move closer and closer to the trunk of the tree until you finally become absorbed into it . . . You are no longer observing the Oak for you are now it. You stand tall and strong. You feel movement in your branches. Listen now to the symphony of

birds, insects, and red squirrels as they play, safe within your fatherly embrace . . . Breathe deeply, purify the air through your leaves . . . Radiate emerald green light so that every living being of the Earth may be healed . . . Become aware of your roots; feel how they reach down into the dark moist soil, spreading far like your branches, anchoring you to the Earth. Experience stillness . . . Only your leaves are stirred by the dance of the warm breeze and the soft summer rain . . .

7. Now it is time gradually to separate your consciousness from that of the tree. Step aside. See that the Oak stands before you. Feel its shelter for a moment before allowing the picture to recede into the distance . . . You are yourself once again.

8. Direct your consciousness back into your body. Imagine yourself centred along a straight line running from the top of your head to your feet . . . Feel safely enclosed within your sphere of light.

9. Open your eyes. Shake out your limbs and have a good stretch from fingertips to toes.

You might also like to meditate on any of the other Flower Remedy plants or trees. Follow the same format as with the Oak meditation. Carry out Steps 1–3, then direct your attention to the subject. First the intellectual consideration: see the plant or tree clearly in your mind; observe it, consider its healing virtues. Then the emotional consideration: reach out to touch the bark of the tree, or the cool silky petals of the flower; smell the scent of Pine or of Honeysuckle. Next, the spiritual consideration: in this phase you become identified with the plant or tree; you are no longer thinking about it because you are it. Finally, disengagement: gradually withdraw from the form of your subject; see it once more as separate from yourself, and then direct your consciousness back into your body as in Steps 7–9.

AND FINALLY . . .

We are all healers, and with love and sympathy in our natures we are also able to help anyone who really desires health. Seek for the outstanding mental conflict in the patient, give him the remedy that will assist him to overcome that particular fault, and all the encouragement and hope you can, and then the healing virtue within him will of itself do the rest.[12]

Dr Edward Bach

Notes

1. Howard, J. and Ramsell, J. *The Original Writings of Edward Bach.*
2. Howard, J. and Ramsell, J. *The Original Writings of Edward Bach.*
3. Chopra, Dr D. *Quantum Healing.*
4. Capra, F. *The Tao of Physics.*
5. Bach, Dr E. *Heal Thyself.*
6. Vlamis, G. *Flowers to the Rescue.*
7. Vlamis, G. *Flowers to the Rescue.*
8. Chancellor, P. *Handbook of the Bach Flower Remedies.*
9. Howard, J. and Ramsell, J. *The Original Writings of Edward Bach.*
10. Wildwood, C. *Aromatherapy.*
11. Bricklin, M. *The Practical Encyclopaedia of Natural Healing.*
12. Howard, J. and Ramsell, J. *The Original Writings of Edward Bach.*

Further Reading

Bach, E. *Heal Thyself*, C.W. Daniel, 1931.

Barnard, J. and Barnard, M. *The Healing Herbs of Edward Bach*, The Flower Remedy Programme, 1988.

Bricklin, Mark, *Practical Encyclopaedia of Natural Healing*, Rodale Press, 1976.

Capra, Dr F. *The Tao of Physics*, Flamingo, 1985.

Chancellor, P.M. *Handbook of the Bach Flower Remedies*, C.W. Daniel, 1971.

Chopra, Dr D. *Quantum Healing*, Bantam Books, 1989.

Howard, J. *The Bach Flower Remedies Step by Step*, C.W. Daniel, 1990.

Howard, J. and Ramsell, J. *The Original Writings of Edward Bach*, C.W. Daniel, 1990.

Kenton, L. *The Biogenic Diet*, Century Arrow, 1986.

Krystal, P. *Cutting The Ties That Bind*, Element Books, 1987.

Scheffer, M. *Bach Flower Therapy*, Thorsons, 1986.

Vlamis, G. *Flowers to the Rescue*, Thorsons, 1986.

Weeks, N. *The Medical Discoveries of Edward Bach, Physician*, C.W. Daniel, 1989.

Wright, C. *The Wright Diet*, Piatkus, 1986.

At a Glance Reference Charts

Summary of uses of flower remedies

WHERE THERE IS doubt, the following reference should serve to elucidate further. However, it is meant as a prompt and should always be used in conjunction with the fuller descriptions presented in Chapter 4.

FLOWER REMEDY	MOOD/PERSONALITY
Agrimony	cheerfulness conceals inner torment; fears being alone; anxious; avoids arguments; rarely complains; weak-willed on occasions; desires excitement; fears illness; restless; sapped by others; suicidal tendencies.
Aspen	fear of some impending evil; delusions; night terrors; suicidal tendencies; ungrounded; sometimes psychic.
Beech	criticizes others; arrogant; has high ideals; irritable; rigid in mind and body; incapable of sympathy for others; strong willed.
Centaury	subservient; a willing drudge; self-denial; conventional; sapped by others; over-sensitive; sometimes mediumistic.
Cerato	always seeking advice; greedy for information; changeable; fussy; saps others; imitative; lacks concentration; conventional; easily dominated; foolish.

At a Glance Reference Chart

FLOWER REMEDY	MOOD/PERSONALITY
Cherry Plum	fears insanity; subject to delusions; feels desperate; has suicidal tendencies; fears harming self or others; nervous breakdown; violent temperament through fear.
Chestnut Bud	fails to learn from past mistakes; lacks observation; a slow learner; thoughts often in the future.
Chicory	possessive (of people and things); dislikes being alone; enjoys arguments; domineering; fussy; mentally congested; fears losing friends; fretful; feigns illness to obtain sympathy; may use emotional blackmail; anxious; self-centred; tearful; strong willed; saps others; house proud.
Clematis	absent minded; daydreams; lacks ambition; apathetic; welcomes prospect of death; ungrounded; lacks vitality; impractical; needs much sleep; imaginative; thoughts in the future; feigns illness to escape from life; sapped by others; uncomplaining; often artistic; sometimes mediumistic.
Crab Apple	self-disgust; over-attention to detail; feels unclean; fussy; house proud; anxious; may have a skin complaint.
Elm	despondent through feelings of inadequacy; feels discouraged though usually copes well.
Gentian	depressed through set-back; 'doubting Thomas' attitude.
Gorse	feels depressed through feelings of hopelessness; can be persuaded to try again, albeit half-heartedly; may be chronically ill.
Heather	self-centred; talkative; saps others; feigns illness to obtain sympathy; dislikes being alone; often lonely; mentally congested; over anxious for self; childish; weeps easily.
Holly	jealous; full of hate; resentful; angry; finds fault with others; violent temperament; suspicious; saps others.
Honeysuckle	nostalgic; lives in the past; absent minded; day dreams; drowsy; homesick; lacks observation; often talkative; sad; saps others.
Hornbeam	uncertain through lack of strength; tired; bored; lazy (that 'Monday morning' feeling).

FLOWER REMEDY	MOOD/PERSONALITY
Impatiens	impatient; irritable; desires to work alone at own swift pace; over-works; has high ideals; self-sufficient; finds fault with others; quick in mind and body; suffers nervous tension; sometimes angry or violent.
Larch	lacks confidence; expects failure; hesitant; feigns illness to avoid responsibility; weak willed; may also suffer from impotency.
Mimulus	nervous by nature; fears known things such as loneliness, poverty, visiting the dentist, animals, parties, speaking in public, etc; shy; lacks confidence; over-sensitive to noise, strife and controversy; has suicidal tendencies; sometimes talkative; sapped by others; easily dominated.
Mustard	feels depression like a black cloud, the cause unknown, often cyclic in nature.
Oak	carries a burden in life; a plodder against all odds; annoyed on account of illness; discontented with self; rarely complains; may suffer nervous breakdown or collapse; violent temperament through instability.
Olive	lacks effort due to physical and emotional exhaustion; fears losing friends; no pleasure in life.
Pine	feels guilt, despair, self-reproach; blames self for the wrong doings of others.
Red Chestnut	over-concern for others; absence of fear for self; always imagines the worst; distressed by reports of war, famine or other disasters; mentally congested; tense.
Rock Rose (also Rescue Remedy)	feels extreme fear, terror or panic — enough to cause fear in those around; nightmares; life or death situations.
Rock Water	hard master to self; self-denial; likes to be a good example to others; self-critical; has fixed ideas and opinions; a perfectionist; intolerant, but rarely openly critical of others; self-martyrdom; anxious; tense; strong willed.

At a Glance Reference Chart

FLOWER REMEDY	MOOD/PERSONALITY
Scleranthus	alternating moods; indecisive; unreliable; lacks concentration; lacks confidence; weak convictions; hesitant; unstable; may suffer nervous breakdown or collapse; lacks poise; restless; may have a violent temperament.
Star of Bethlehem (also Rescue Remedy)	emotional and physical shock; deep-rooted problems due to past trauma; grief; emotional numbness; refuses to be consoled; tense.
Sweet Chestnut	extreme anguish, so great as to seem unbearable; utter despair; unable even to pray.
Vervain	over-enthusiastic; missionary zeal; enjoys argument and debate; strong willed; interferes in the affairs of others; over-effort; rigid in mind and body; impulsive; intolerant; a martyr to the cause; may suffer nervous breakdown or collapse; nervy; quick in mind and body; talkative.
Vine	dictatorial; ruthlessly ambitious; strong willed; hard master to others; intolerant; lacks sympathy for others; violent temperament; born to lead.
Walnut	difficulty in severing old ties; has definite ambition; finds transition difficult; sometimes held back or misguided by others; feels frustration.
Water Violet	proud and aloof; suffers in silence; physical rigidity; self-reliant; desires to be alone; avoids argument; poised; sad; radiates superiority.
White Chestnut	tormented by mental arguments; carousel mind; may suffer from insomnia; lacks observation; worried.
Wild Oat	dissatisfaction through unfulfilled ambition; uncertain about the future; sometimes a 'Jack of all trades, master of none'; unable to settle down.
Wild Rose	apathetic (the cause often unknown); weary; gloomy; uncomplaining; dislikes change; 'I'll have to live with it' attitude.
Willow	'poor me' attitude; bitter and resentful; selfish; enjoys arguments; blames others; grumpy; morose; may simulate illness to obtain pity; irritable; sulky.

Finding a flower remedy for your mental state

A s WITH the previous chart, the following reference will serve as a useful prompt, but should always be used in conjunction with the flower essence profiles in Chapter 4.

MENTAL STATE	POSSIBLE FLOWER REMEDIES
Absent-Mindedness	Chestnut Bud, Clematis, Honeysuckle, Mustard, Olive, White Chestnut, Wild Rose
Addiction (to substances/limitation/individuals)	Agrimony, Aspen, Chestnut Bud, Clematis
Aggression	Cherry Plum, Holly, Impatiens, Rescue Remedy, Scleranthus, Vine
Aloofness	Rock Water, Water Violet
Ambivalence	Cerato, Scleranthus, Wild Oat
Anger	Cherry Plum, Holly, Impatiens, Rescue Remedy, Vine
Anxiety	Agrimony, Aspen, Cerato, Chicory, Cherry Plum, Crab Apple, Elm, Heather, Larch, Mimulus, Red Chestnut, Rescue Remedy, Rock Water, White Chestnut
Apathy	Clematis, Gorse, Wild Rose
Argumentativeness	Beech, Chicory, Holly, Impatiens, Vervain, Vine, Willow
Arrogance	Beech, Vine
Bemused, Feeling of being	Clematis, Rescue Remedy
Boredom	Hornbeam
Broken-Heartedness	Clematis, Holly, Honeysuckle, Rescue Remedy, Star of Bethlehem, Sweet Chestnut, Wild Rose, Willow
Confidence, Lack of	Cerato, Centaury, Elm, Larch, Pine

At A Glance Reference Charts

MENTAL STATE	POSSIBLE FLOWER REMEDIES
Delusions	Aspen, Cherry Plum, Rescue Remedy
Devitalization	Olive
Depression	Gentian, Gorse, Mustard, Sweet Chestnut, Wild Rose
Despondency and Despair	Crab Apple, Elm, Larch, Oak, Pine, Star of Bethlehem, Sweet Chestnut, Willow
Disdainfulness	Beech, Crab Apple, Rock Water, Water Violet
Disorientation	Clematis, Honeysuckle, Rescue Remedy, Scleranthus
Domineering, Desire to be	Chicory, Vervain, Vine
Egotism	Beech, Chicory, Holly, Water Violet
Easily Led, Being	Agrimony, Centaury, Cerato, Chestnut Bud, Walnut
Emotional Blackmail (to obtain pity)	Chicory, Willow
Escapism	Agrimony, Clematis, Chestnut Bud, Honeysuckle, Water Violet, Wild Oat
Fanaticism	Vervain, Vine
Fear	Aspen, Cherry Plum, Mimulus, Red Chestnut, Rescue Remedy, Rock Rose
Frustration	Gentian, Impatiens
Fussiness	Cerato, Chicory, Crab Apple, Beech
Grief (see *Broken-Heartedness*)	
Guilt	Pine
Hatred	Holly, Willow
Homesickness	Honeysuckle
Hopelessness	Gorse, Sweet Chestnut, Wild Rose

MENTAL STATE	POSSIBLE FLOWER REMEDIES
Hysteria	Rescue Remedy, Rock Rose
Idealism	Elm, Rock Water, Vervain
Impulsiveness	Impatiens, Vervain
Inertia	Chestnut Bud, Hornbeam
Intolerance	Beech, Impatiens, Rock Water, Vervain, Vine, Willow
Insecurity	Aspen, Larch, Mimulus, Wild Oat
Imitative, Being	Cerato
Indecisiveness	Cerato, Larch, Scleranthus, Wild Oat
Inner Torment	Agrimony
Insomnia (see also *Worry*)	Rescue Remedy, White Chestnut
Irritability	Beech, Chicory, Crab Apple, Impatiens, Willow
Jealousy	Holly
Loneliness	Beech, Chicory, Elm, Heather, Holly, Honeysuckle, Impatiens, Mustard, Sweet Chestnut, Water Violet
Mental Congestion	Heather, Rescue Remedy, White Chestnut
Miserliness	Chicory, Willow
Mood-Swings	Rescue Remedy, Scleranthus
Monotonous Existence	Centaury, Gentian, Wild Rose
Nervous Breakdown	Cherry Plum, Oak, Rescue Remedy, Vervain
Nervy, Being	Aspen, Cherry Plum, Impatiens, Mimulus, Rescue Remedy, Vervain
Nightmares	Aspen, Cherry Plum, Rescue Remedy, Rock Rose
Nostalgia	Honeysuckle

MENTAL STATE	POSSIBLE FLOWER REMEDIES
Over-Critical, Tendency to being	Beech, Chicory, Vine
Over-Sensitivity	Aspen, Beech, Centaury, Crab Apple, Mimulus, Red Chestnut, Rescue Remedy, Star of Bethlehem, Walnut
Overwhelmed, Feeling of being	Cherry Plum, Elm, Hornbeam, Oak, Rescue Remedy, Sweet Chestnut
Overwork	Elm, Impatiens, Oak, Rescue Remedy
Paranoia	Aspen, Holly
Perfectionism	Agrimony, Beech, Crab Apple, Elm, Rock Water, Water Violet
Pessimism	Gentian, Gorse, Larch
Phobias	Mimulus, Rescue Remedy
Possessiveness	Chicory, Heather, Red Chestnut
Procrastination	Cerato, Scleranthus
Psychism, Uncontrolled	Aspen, Clematis, Rescue Remedy
Rejection, Feelings of	Chicory, Crab Apple, Holly, Honeysuckle, Larch, Pine, Sweet Chestnut, Willow
Resentfulness	Beech, Chicory, Holly, Willow
Restlessness	Agrimony, Impatiens, Vervain, White Chestnut, Wild Oat
Sapped by Others, Being	Agrimony, Centaury, Clematis, Mimulus
Sap Others, Tendency to	Cerato, Chicory, Heather, Holly, Honeysuckle
Self-Aggrandizement	Beech, Vine, Water Violet
Self-Centredness	Beech, Chicory, Heather, Vine, Willow
Self-Criticism	Crab Apple, Rock Water
Self-Deception	Agrimony

MENTAL STATE	POSSIBLE FLOWER REMEDIES
Self-Disgust	Crab Apple
Self-Effacement	Centaury, Pine
Selfishness	Chicory, Heather, Holly
Self-Martyrdom	Centaury, Rock Water
Self-Pity	Chicory, Willow
Shame	Agrimony, Crab Apple, Larch, Pine
Shock	Rescue Remedy, Star of Bethlehem
Stress	Cherry Plum, Elm, Impatiens, Olive, Rescue Remedy, Star of Bethlehem, Vervain
Subservience	Centaury
Suicidal Tendencies	Agrimony, Cherry Plum, Mimulus, Rescue Remedy
Suppressed Emotion	Agrimony, Beech, Rock Water, Water Violet
Suspiciousness	Holly
Temper Tantrum	Cherry Plum, Holly, Impatiens, Rescue Remedy
Tension	Impatiens, Rescue Remedy, Rock Water, Vervain, Water Violet
Uncertainty	Cerato, Scleranthus
Unfulfilled Ambition	Walnut, Wild Oat
Unconsciousness	Clematis, Rescue Remedy
Ungroundedness	Aspen, Cherry Plum, Clematis, Honeysuckle, Mimulus, Rescue Remedy, Rock Rose, Scleranthus, Star of Bethlehem, Walnut
Unsympathetic, Feeling	Beech, Vine, Willow
Violent Actions, Thoughts or Dreams	Cherry Plum, Holly, Impatiens, Scleranthus, Rescue Remedy, Vine
Weak Will	Agrimony, Centaury, Cerato, Larch, Mimulus

MENTAL STATE	POSSIBLE FLOWER REMEDIES
Worry	Agrimony, Aspen, Crab Apple, Elm, Gentian, Mimulus, Mustard, Oak, Red Chestnut, Rescue Remedy, White Chestnut

Useful Addresses

SUPPLIERS OF BOOKS and Flower Remedies (mail order). Please enclose a stamped addressed envelope with all enquiries:

The Bach Centre,
Mount Vernon,
Sotwell,
Wallingford,
Oxfordshire, OX10 OPZ
GB
Tel: 01491–39489/34678

The Flower Remedy Programme,
PO Box 65,
Hereford, HR2 OUW
GB

Although the above organization has no connection with the Bach Centre in Oxfordshire, their Flower Remedies are prepared from the same plant species, employing the traditional methods as advocated by Dr Bach.

Other official distributors of the Bach Centre are:

USA/Canada

Ellon (Bach USA) Inc.,
PO Box 320,
Woodmere,
NY 11598,
Tel: 516–825–2229

Australia

Martin & Pleasance Wholesale Pty Ltd.,
PO Box 4,
Collingwood,
Victoria 3066
Tel: 419–9733

Nonesuch Botanicals Pty Ltd.,
PO Box 68,
Mt Evelyn,
Victoria 3796
Tel: 762–8577

Holland

Holland Pharma,
Postbus 37,
7240 AA Lochem
Tel: 05730–2884

Denmark

Camette,
Murervej 16,
6700 Esbjerg
Tel: 05–155444

Germany, Austria, Switzerland

Mechthild Scheffer HP,
Bach Centre – German Office,
Eppendorfer Landstrasse 32,
2000 Hamburg 20
Tel: 040–46 10 41

New Zealand

Ushers Odeon Pharmacy,
Tutanakai Street,
Rotorua,
New Zealand
Tel. 64 87 765

For those in need of counselling, psychotherapy, or spiritual healing, contact the following organization. Courses and workshops are also available. Please enclose a stamped addressed envelope with all enquiries.

The Pegasus Foundation,
Runnings Park,
Croft Bank,
West Malvern,
Worcestershire, WR14 4DU
GB

For spiritual healing only, write to the following organization. They will supply the name, address, and telephone number of an accredited healer in your area.

National Federation of Spiritual Healers,
Old Manor Farm Studio,
Church Street,
Sunbury-on-Thames,
Middlesex, TW16 6RG
GB

Index